Head, Shoulders, Pee, and Moles

An Eyes-and-Ears-and-Mouth-and-Nose Guide to SELF-DIAGNOSIS

Paul Kleinman

Technical Review by
Carolyn Dean, MD, ND

Avon, Massachusetts

I would like to thank the guy who first thought of
attaching a bottle of hand sanitizer to a carabiner.
I don't know who you are, but you're my hero.

Published by
Adams Media, a division of F+W Media, Inc.
57 Littlefield Street, Avon, MA 02322. U.S.A.
www.adamsmedia.com

ISBN 10: 1-4405-3363-6
ISBN 13: 978-1-4405-3363-1
eISBN 10: 1-4405-3952-9
eISBN 13: 978-1-4405-3952-7

Printed in the United States of America.

10   9   8   7   6   5   4   3   2   1

Library of Congress Cataloging-in-Publication Data
is available from the publisher.

This publication is designed to provide accurate and authoritative information with regard to the subject matter covered. It is sold with the understanding that the publisher is not engaged in rendering legal, accounting, or other professional advice. If legal advice or other expert assistance is required, the services of a competent professional person should be sought.
—From a *Declaration of Principles* jointly adopted by a Committee of the American Bar Association and a Committee of Publishers and Associations

Many of the designations used by manufacturers and sellers to distinguish their product are claimed as trademarks. Where those designations appear in this book and Adams Media was aware of a trademark claim, the designations have been printed with initial capital letters.

This book is intended as general information only, and should not be used to diagnose or treat any health condition. In light of the complex, individual, and specific nature of health problems, this book is not intended to replace professional medical advice. The ideas, procedures, and suggestions in this book are intended to supplement, not replace, the advice of a trained medical professional. Consult your physician before adopting any of the suggestions in this book, as well as about any condition that may require diagnosis or medical attention. The author and publisher disclaim any liability arising directly or indirectly from the use of this book.

This book is available at quantity discounts for bulk purchases.
For information, please call 1-800-289-0963.

Contents

Introduction • 5

Part 1

The Head • 7

Chapter 1: Hair • 8

Chapter 2: Scalp • 13

Chapter 3: Face • 19

Chapter 4: Eyes • 28

Chapter 5: Ears • 38

Chapter 6: Nose • 44

Chapter 7: Mouth • 51

Chapter 8: Neck • 62

Part 2

The Torso • 69

Chapter 9: Skin • 70

Chapter 10: Shoulders • 90

Chapter 11: Back • 96

Chapter 12: Arms • 105

Chapter 13: Hands • 121

Chapter 14: Fingers • 129

Chapter 15: Chest • 138

Chapter 16: Breasts • 143

Chapter 17: Stomach • 152

Chapter 18: Pelvis • 160

Chapter 19: Buttocks • 180

Part 3

The Legs and Feet • 189

Chapter 20: Legs • 190

Chapter 21: Feet • 206

Chapter 22: Toes • 212

Index • 219

Introduction

They say what doesn't kill you makes you stronger. I say what doesn't kill you . . . doesn't exist.

Fellow hypochondriacs, neurotics, worrywarts, germaphobes, and self-diagnosing paranoid people, lend me your clean and disinfected ears! Are you tired of spending your days by the computer, reading webpage after webpage in a desperate attempt to find out what is wrong with you? Do you often hear people tell you to get out more or ask you when was the last time you went outside? Has anyone ever told you to not worry so much or that you should just touch the stupid subway pole because it's not going to kill you? Well, with this book, you can do all of that! And more! Gone are the days where you type symptoms into a search bar and browse through your results. No longer will each click of the mouse jangle a new and different set of nerves! No Internet? No problem! You don't need the Internet to take care of your self-diagnosing needs! All you'll ever need is the information you'll find here!

Right now you're probably thinking to yourself, "Can this book really be better than the Internet when it comes to researching my symptoms? Will I be able to find out useful information about medical disorders and conditions? Can this book help me identify the cause of a rash, lump, or deformity on any particular part of my body? What if I have pseudomonas folliculitis or something? Would the book be able to inform me of this?" Well, dear reader, yes, yes, yes, and, yes! (And it might be a good idea to stay out of the hot tub for a while . . .)

This book will go over various parts of your body in detail and describe what different symptoms and signs may mean. And to top it all off, this information is completely medically accurate and has been reviewed by an actual doctor and naturopath. That's right, I said reviewed by a doctor. You know, those people who are sick of seeing you at their office every day. Those people who have read about even more illnesses than you. In other words, what you hold in your hands is a hypochondriac's dream come true. So have a seat; get out your hand sanitizer; make sure your physician, dermatologist, and allergist are on speed dial; and find your happy place, because it's time to start self-diagnosing. And really, no matter what anyone tells you, those subway poles are seriously a breeding ground for disease.

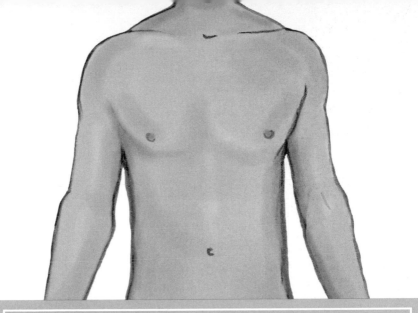

Part 1

The Head

Hair • Scalp • Face • Eyes • Ears • Nose • Mouth • Neck

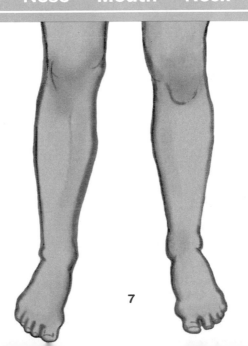

7

CHAPTER 1

Hair

Your hair can tell a lot about you, and it has nothing to do with the way you style it. Are you going prematurely gray? Is your hair dry and brittle? Is it falling out in patches? Is it falling out everywhere? What your hair looks and feels like can actually inform you of certain health problems, and sometimes the signs can be as subtle as that pitch-black mohawk you sported as a teenager. So if your hair is talking to you, you'd better listen up! If you don't treat your hair properly now, the only style you'll be showing off in the long run is a baseball cap and shiny scalp.

IF YOUR HAIR . . .

. . . falls out all over

You may be overstressed. Diffuse hair loss is a symptom of telogen effluvium, a common disorder caused by hormones kicked up by big changes in people's lives. Just about anything worrying can start it, from a single distressing event—like a death in the family—to more prolonged, daily anxiety caused by the economy, work, or chronic illness. A most indiscriminate and nonfatal condition, it can occur in men and women of any age or race. You may notice an unusual amount of hair on your brush, in the shower drain trap, or falling freely when you run your hand through your hair. Depending on the trigger, it can be acute and reverse itself within six months or it can be chronic and persistent. General medical treatment of acute cases recommends stress-relief exercises, patience, and a big hat if you're really that embarrassed.

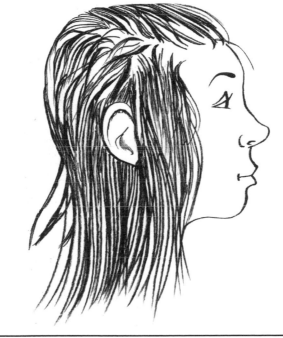

Telogen effluvium

. . . falls out in patches

You may be experiencing symptoms of cicatricial alopecia or alopecia areata. If the cause is cicatricial alopecia, you must treat any inflammation immediately as it causes scarring that will prevent your hair from growing back. Alopecia areata, an autoimmune disorder often linked to thyroid diseases, is less serious; though you will lose your hair, it will eventually grow back. You may also be experiencing male- or female-pattern baldness, in which case it's wise to stock up on the usual hair regeneration shampoo—or at least a classy wig or toupee.

. . . is dry and brittle

You may be anorexic, bulimic, or experiencing symptoms of hypothyroidism or hypoparathyroidism. In hypothyroidism, the body is less capable of metabolizing food and creating energy, which dries out your skin and hair. In hypoparathyroidism, calcium levels fall and phosphorous levels rise due to a lack of the parathyroid hormone, which regulates the calcium and phosphorus levels in extracellular fluid. This drop in calcium, especially if you also have poor absorption of vitamin D, dries out your hair. If you're suffering from anorexia or bulimia, you're not ingesting enough or you're throwing up, so your body isn't getting enough of the nutrients, proteins, and omega-3 fatty acids that it needs. This lack of nutrients is responsible for making your hair dry and brittle. One way or another, you're not getting enough of something, whether it's hormones, nutrients, or moisturizing shampoo.

This lack of nutrients is responsible for making your hair dry and brittle.

. . . seems thicker

If you're a woman, you may be pregnant. In a normal hair cycle, your hair grows about half an inch per month for two to six years. Then your hair will rest for around two or three months, and fall out. At any time, 90 percent of the hair on your head is in the growing phase and 10 percent of your hair is in the resting phase. When a woman becomes pregnant, the percent of hair in the resting phase can increase by up to 60 percent. This means less hair falls out, and you start looking like you belong in a shampoo commercial. Of course, pregnancy hormones can also give you hair in places you never had hair before, like your stomach, back, and breasts. After giving birth, the resting phase of your hair will become shorter and it may appear as though your hair is thinner than normal (because more hair is falling out). As your new hair grows in, your hair cycle will become normal again, which is something you won't be able to say about your sleep cycle.

. . . is growing in places that it shouldn't grow

If you're a woman, you may have what is known as hirsutism. This is when women have male-pattern hair growth, such as coarse, pigmented hair growing on the face, back, and chest. Hirsutism may be caused by a family trait or by excess androgens (male hormones) such as testosterone. When extremely high levels of androgens are enough to cause hirsutism, other symptoms may appear in a process known as virilization. These symptoms can include acne, balding, a decrease in the size of the breasts, a deepening of the voice, an increase in muscle mass, and an enlarged clitoris. If this happens to you, look on the bright side; you can always start a new career as a bearded lady.

. . . is prematurely gray

According to traditional Chinese medicine, this could mean that you have a kidney meridian imbalance. In this practice, the kidney is responsible for maturation, development, reproduction, and growth, and is connected to the bones, the ears, the teeth, and the hair on your head. Other symptoms of a kidney imbalance include hair loss, dry mouth, osteoporosis, night sweats, pain in your lower back, hearing loss or a ringing in your ears, frequent urination, incontinence, and having a bad short-term memory. If I had all of those symptoms, I think my hair would go prematurely gray, too.

> **Do you chemically treat your hair?**
> If you do, you may be more likely to be diagnosed with cancer. Many popular straightening treatments include high levels of carcinogenic formaldehyde, and dark dyes have been shown to increase rates of bladder cancer in hairdressers. If you start going through stylists as quickly as cancer studies go through lab rats, you might have a problem.

. . . has a band that is discolored or depigmented

You may have a protein or iron deficiency. A band or stripe of discolored hair (usually reddish, blonde, or gray in color) can also be a rare indication of ulcerative colitis (an inflammatory bowel disease that creates inflammation in the lining of the rectum or colon), anorexia, or other illnesses where protein is depleted from the body. A discolored stripe of hair due to protein or iron deficiency is much more common in people living in underdeveloped countries, but bands of red, blonde, or gray hair can also be found in the indigenous "Hipster" people found in Williamsburg, Brooklyn.

CHAPTER 2

Scalp

Are you flakey? Have you ever experienced a real head-scratcher? I'm not talking about your IQ; I'm talking about the top of your head. A bad case of flaking, scaling, or crusting won't only lead to discomfort, itching, and pain, but it can turn you into a social pariah faster than you can say "pityriasis capitis." If you ever want to regain your social life, you're going to need to start taking care of your scalp. Even flakey people can start making smart decisions every now and then . . .

IF YOUR SCALP . . .

. . . flakes

You, my friend, are most likely suffering from pityriasis capitis, or as it is more commonly known, dandruff. Don't worry, though; this happens to just about everyone. As the skin renews itself, dead skin cells fall off and are replaced by new ones. This process occurs quicker in people who have dandruff, and more skin cells are shed. This leads to the visibly white clumps or flakes you find on your dark clothing. Dandruff, contrary to popular belief, is not a result of dry skin but rather the result of very oily skin. It is caused by *Malassezia furfur*, a fungus that happens to be present in every person's scalp. Everything from allergic reactions, UV light, seasonal changes, and emotional stress can lead to dandruff. Some people believe the way to prevent dandruff is to stop washing their hair with shampoo or to wash less frequently, but actually they should be washing with antifungal or antidandruff shampoo. So brush those flakes off your black shirt and get in the shower!

Malassezia furfur

... is crusty or scaly

You may have scalp psoriasis or seborrheic dermatitis. Both conditions lead to itching, and, in cases of seborrheic dermatitis, it can be severe. To help distinguish between the two, it is important to understand the symptoms. Scalp psoriasis features red patches that have silvery scales; dry patches that appear on other parts of the body such as your hands, feet, knees, and elbows; crust or scaling that might bleed when removed; and silvery scales that can attach to hair shafts. Seborrheic dermatitis features greasy yellow or white scales covering red and oily skin, crust or scales that can be removed easily, patches that do not move past the hairline, and white or yellow scales that can attach to hair shafts. When a snake sheds its skin, it's cool looking. When you do it, not so much.

. . . is red

You may have scalp psoriasis, seborrheic dermatitis (see previous entry), or atopic eczema. Though atopic eczema is most commonly found in children, it can occur in adults as well. A person with atopic eczema has dry and red skin. As the condition flares up, your skin might swell up and small water blisters will develop. If scratched, these blisters will ooze, and your skin might flake and thicken. Those with asthma or hay fever are more likely to get atopic eczema and vice versa. The condition can be caused from reactions to things like dust mites, pollen, fragrances added in soaps and perfumes, stress, water, being sick or having the flu, and feeling very hot or very cold. Other reasons for red scalp include sunburns and painting your head red to attend a game involving your favorite sports team. Unfortunately, there's no treatment for fanaticism if your team sucks.

. . . has small bumps

You may simply have scalp acne or an ingrown hair. Other reasons for small bumps on your scalp include seborrheic dermatitis or scalp folliculitis. Essentially, scalp folliculitis occurs when a hair follicle becomes infected and there is an inflammatory reaction. For many, this can happen on a regular basis and can become a nuisance. Perifolliculitis capitis abscedens et suffodiens, or PCAS, is a rare and extreme form of scalp folliculitis and features large cysts or nodules with small pustules and papules that can lead to temporary hair loss and permanent bald patches and scarring. Most often, black adult men are affected with perifolliculitis capitis abscedens et suffodiens. Though, it should also be noted that men and women of all races have difficulty saying the name and give up halfway through.

. . . has one large bump

It can mean you have a pilar cyst, also known as a sebaceous cyst, seborrheic keratosis, or even skin cancer. Pilar cysts, which are white or skin-colored, can appear anywhere on your scalp and usually do not hurt. They consist of dead skin cells and oil, and can grow to the size of a tangerine. Seborrheic keratosis is a benign skin tumor that grows on the top of your scalp and is beige, gray, or brown in color. If irritated, it can itch and bleed. Skin cancer can be found on any part of the scalp. A melanoma appears as a small dark mole, basal cell carcinoma can appear as a waxy or pearly bump, and squamous cell skin cancer can appear as a red nodule that is firm. It is also possible that the large bump is a result of a trauma. Such traumas to the head can be prevented by ducking, looking up as you walk, and not inviting your ex over for dinner to discuss "where things went wrong."

. . . has scars and inflamed bumps

You probably have acne keloidalis nuchae, a type of chronic folliculitis (otherwise known as swollen hair follicles). The condition begins as red bumps filled with pus that are usually itchy or tender. The term *nuchae* means nape of neck, which gives you a clue to the location of these bumps that form on the lower part of the scalp or on the back of the neck. As time progresses, small scars will develop from these bumps. If this is left untreated, the small scars can combine to form keloids, scars that are large and thick. These keloids then lead to hair loss and permanent scarring. Acne keloidalis nuchae occurs most frequently in young black males and rarely occurs after middle age or before puberty. Acne keloidalis nuchae is not actually related to acne vulgaris (otherwise known as acne), but the lesions do appear similar to acne in the beginning. And while acne keloidalis nuchae sure sounds bad, the fact that it can permanently put an end to mullets is rather appealing . . .

. . . itches

You may have seborrheic dermatitis, scalp psoriasis, folliculitis, a fungal or bacterial infection, a sunburn, atopic eczema, an allergic reaction to anything used topically (including a hat), lupus, hypothyroidism, or head lice. An itchy scalp can also be caused by anxiety and stress (and really, who wouldn't be anxious and stressed out after reading all of that?). An itchy scalp can lead to lesions and open sores, bald patches, thinning hair, hair loss, and infections. If your scalp is constantly itching, it's best to have your dermatologist determine the root of the problem because your itchiness may be a symptom for an underlying disease or condition. After all, how do you expect to nervously pull the hair out of your head if there's no hair there in the first place?

> An itchy scalp can lead to lesions and open sores . . . thinning hair, hair loss, and infections.

. . . has a mushy part with pus-filled bumps

You may have a kerion, which develops following a severe case of ringworm on the scalp. Sometimes, a person who has a kerion also suffers from a fever. While ringworm of the scalp is generally a harmless condition, if the fungal infection turns into a kerion, you can end up with permanent hair loss and scarring. The easiest way to develop ringworm on the scalp is by direct contact with someone—either human or animal—who is infected or by touching a contaminated object (such as a brush, comb, or pillow). Kerions are most often seen in children; however, there have been cases of adults with the condition although it often goes undiagnosed. It is believed that kerions are the result of an allergic reaction to the fungus that causes ringworm or from an overactive immune system. Who knew that an overactive immune system could be a bad thing?

CHAPTER 3

Face

Come face to face with illness like you never thought possible! Sure, having electric shocklike pains, a butterfly-shaped rash, shiny skin that can't move, or partial facial paralysis is pretty terrifying, but the causes of these conditions are maybe even more frightening! So if you have any of the symptoms discussed in this chapter, tell someone about it now—while you can still move your face.

IF YOUR FACE . . .

. . . is dry

It could be due to a number of reasons. Dry weather with low humidity, bathing too much, not drinking enough water, and getting sunburned can all lead to dry skin. Taking antihistamines, diuretics, smoking, drinking alcohol, and even having caffeine can disrupt your body's pH levels, also leading to dry skin. Omega-3 fatty acids, vitamin A, B complex, and zinc play key roles in maintaining your skin structure, so if you lack any of these, your skin may begin to dry out. Dry skin can also be a sign of hypothyroidism, where the activity of your sweat and oil glands is reduced due to the thyroid producing too few hormones. Lastly, as you age, your body's oil-producing glands naturally start to become less active, leading to dryer and rougher skin. You may look more hydrated than King Tut, but at least he aged well!

. . . is swollen

You may have an infection, inflammation, allergic reaction, cancer, or have suffered some sort of trauma. Facial swelling, also known as facial edema, is most noticeable on the eyelids, lips, and cheeks. If swelling occurs over a period of time and occurs with other symptoms like congestion and pain, it might be an infection such as sinusitis. Other infectious causes of facial edema include the mumps, cellulitis, viral or bacterial conjunctivitis, and a sty. Allergic reactions; failure of the heart, liver, and kidneys; and severe malnutrition can also lead to swelling of the face. Facial edema can lead to difficulty in breathing, respiratory arrest, spread of infection to other parts of your body, tissue or skin removal, and even loss of vision. A swollen head does not mean that you are smarter than other people, but that sort of cockiness can certainly lead to someone giving you a facial swelling.

> Facial swelling, also known as facial edema, is most noticeable on the eyelids, lips, and cheeks.

. . . has round, itchy, burning, and swollen areas or welts

You may have hives. Hives occur when the body encounters something it perceives as dangerous and releases histamine to counterattack and fight the allergen off. Common triggers of hives include pollen; ragweed; grasses; trees; food allergies; exposure to sunlight; insect bites and stings; overexposure to hot and/or cold temperatures; overexposure to water; allergic reactions to drugs, soaps, and shampoos; and certain diseases and infections like leukemia and lupus. Many people who experience hives on their face can also experience angioedema, a swelling similar to hives that is present underneath the skin. Without the proper treatment, hives on your face can recur on a regular basis. Often hives are passed on to future generations. And really, with that receding hairline and the "family" nose, don't you have enough to pass on to your kids?

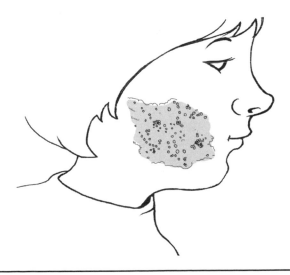

Hives

. . . is red

You may have a skin disease known as rosacea. People with rosacea have pimples and redness around their nose, forehead, cheeks, and chin, and have tiny veins on their face that look similar to spider webs. The redness is caused by the expansion of blood vessels located in the face and can sometimes last for days. This is often triggered by sunlight, wind, spicy foods, alcohol, hot weather, exercise, and extreme changes in weather; in fact, anything that heats up your face or increases circulation can trigger symptoms. Other symptoms of the condition include swollen eyelids and dry, irritated, and red eyes. If a serious case of rosacea is left untreated, it can create bumps on your nose and cheeks that will spread, and, eventually, your face may appear swollen and waxy (this state of rosacea is known as rhinophyma). On the one hand, you'll probably get stared at by people as you walk by. But on a more positive note, you'd be able to moonlight as a figurine in a wax museum.

. . . has a rapidly growing, volcanic-looking bump

You may have a keratoacanthoma, which is a less severe type of squamous cell carcinoma. Usually keratoacanthoma appears in parts of the skin that are exposed to the most sunlight, such as the face and neck, and generally these bumps appear in middle-aged people and the elderly. Keratoacanthomas develop and grow very quickly. It usually takes only two to six weeks for one to appear and grow to its full size. Following this, the keratoacanthoma will remain dormant for another two to six weeks, and then over a course of two to twelve months it will regress, heal, and leave a scar. While having many keratoacanthomas can be a sign of Muir-Torre syndrome—a type of cancer that features skin lesions and cancers of the breast, genitourinary tract, and colon—these bumps are generally benign. This does not mean that keratoacanthomas should go untreated, because it can be difficult to distinguish a keratoacanthoma from squamous cell carcinoma, and sometimes a keratoacanthoma can become a squamous cell carcinoma. So do yourself a favor and get checked out by a dermatologist . . . Or a volcanologist. Whichever one is easier.

Hey, Bighead!

Studies have shown that people with larger heads are actually smarter and have better memory than their small-headed counterparts. Being born with a big head isn't necessarily important, but by the time you are about one year old (the formative years of your brain), the size of your head will help determine your intelligence later on in life. And when you are older, the larger your head is, the less memory decline you will have. While the cause of why one baby's head might become larger than another baby's head is unknown, scientists believe that the relationship between child and parent plays an important role, and that a stimulating and intellectual environment may lead to a baby's head growing. Parents always seem to think that their child is a little genius, and if they care for him correctly, they might just create one—but they'll still have a hard time shopping for hats.

. . . has stabbing, electric-shocklike pains

You might be experiencing a nerve disorder known as trigeminal neuralgia. The pain you are experiencing is from the trigeminal nerve, which is responsible for carrying sensations such as pain and feeling from the brain to the skin of the face. Trigeminal neuralgia can be a result of a tumor or swollen blood vessel that applies pressure to the trigeminal nerve, or it can be a result of multiple sclerosis, a debilitating disorder where the body's immune system attacks the protective covering of the nerve cells (known as the myelin sheath), and leads to irreversible deterioration of the nerves. But more common reasons for trigeminal neuralgia are exposure to a cold draft on the face, a viral infection of the nerve as in shingles due to chickenpox, a dental infection, or eye strain. The stabbing pain can be triggered by everyday events such as brushing your teeth, eating, drinking, shaving, and even by noises and gentle touches. The pain is usually located on one side, around the lower area of the face, as well as around the eye and cheek. The painful spasms can last anywhere from a few seconds to a few minutes and can become frequent. Oh, and one last thing, trigeminal neuralgia is also a normal part of the aging process. So while your legs will move slower, at least your nerves will transmit that pain with lightning speed. Isn't that comforting?

> The painful spasms can last anywhere from a few seconds to a few minutes and can become frequent.

... has dark discoloration

You may have a skin disorder called melasma. Usually, the browning of the skin on the face is symmetrical, meaning it matches on both sides, and it occurs on the forehead, cheeks, upper lip, and nose. Melasma is particularly common in women who are pregnant (so common, in fact, that it is referred to as the "mask of pregnancy") and women who take birth control pills or take hormone replacement therapy. The brown color usually begins to fade within a few months of having your child or stopping the medication that is causing it. The biggest way to prevent melasma from occurring is by avoiding the sun and protecting your skin with sunscreen—especially if you are hormonally challenged. If you have melasma, you should reapply sunscreen every two hours . . . and consider moving underground.

. . . has a rash that starts at one cheek, goes over the nose, and ends at the other cheek

You may have systemic lupus erythematosus, or more simply, lupus. Lupus is a chronic inflammatory disease where the body actually attacks its own healthy tissues and organs. Many different parts of the body can be affected by lupus, including the skin, kidneys, joints, blood cells, heart, brain, and lungs. While lupus can be difficult to diagnose because its symptoms can resemble other conditions and vary from person to person, the butterfly rash around the nose and cheeks is one of the only very distinctive symptoms of lupus. Lupus is much more common in women, and Asian and black people are affected more often than people of other races. Though the cause of lupus remains unknown, it is believed that some are born with a predisposition to the illness, and certain things like sunlight and medications can trigger it. Of course, that rash might just be from spending too much time outside in the sun, but you should check in with your doctor anyway. A sunburn is one thing, but a chronic inflammatory disease that attacks your insides is another thing all together.

> The body actually attacks its own healthy tissues and organs.

> ## Your face can tell a lot about you . . .
>
> In ayurvedic medicine, it is believed that the face mirrors the mind and that illness and disease of the body will manifest itself on the face in one way or another. If you have fluffy and full lower eyelids, this could be a sign of impaired kidneys. If you have a butterfly-like discoloration appearing on your cheeks or on your nose, this may mean that you have malabsorption of folic acid or iron or that you may have lupus. The wrinkles you have on your head are also believed to have particular meanings. If you have a wrinkle that is a vertical line between your eyebrows and on the right side, this means that you have suppressed emotions in your liver. If you have a wrinkle that is a horizontal line between your eyebrows and it is on the left side, this means that your spleen has suppressed emotions. If this sounds like you, get that spleen to a therapist who will encourage it to talk about its feelings, and say goodbye to that little line!

. . . is paralyzed or weak on one side

You may have a condition known as Bell's palsy. The main symptom of the condition is a sudden paralysis or weakness on one side of your face caused by damage to the nerve responsible for controlling your facial muscles. This damage is due to inflammation, which can be caused by a viral infection from HIV, Epstein-Barr or herpes zoster (shingles), sarcoidosis, or Lyme disease. The damaged nerve causes the side of your face to droop. It can also lead to a numbness of the affected side, drooling, pain behind or in the ear, and eye problems. Though still unclear, it is believed that the herpes virus responsible for cold sores can also cause Bell's palsy. The condition usually occurs overnight and is usually triggered by stress or reactivation of a virus; it typically heals on its own within a couple of months. It is important to know that Bell's palsy is in no way linked to a transient ischemic attack or stroke, which involve a disruption of blood flow to the brain. So if you're ever on a date, you can just say, "Oh, no. Don't worry. The droopy face thing goes away. The herpes on the other hand . . . "

. . . has tight, shiny skin that can't move

This is a symptom of a series of progressive diseases known as scleroderma. Scleroderma involves the tightening and hardening of a person's connective tissues and skin, and while some types only affect the skin, others can affect the heart, digestive tract, kidneys, and lungs. Other symptoms of scleroderma include Raynaud's phenomenon—which is a color change, numbness, and pain in the fingers and toes from cold temperature or emotional distress—acid reflux, gastroesophageal reflux disease (where food regurgitates from your stomach because your muscles are rigid and don't move food down through your intestines properly), and thick, oval-shaped patches of white skin with a purple border especially on your fingers. Though the cause is unknown, scleroderma is a result of the body producing too much collagen in the tissues of the body. But don't think of your scleroderma as debilitating; just think of it as a poor-gal's Botox!

Scleroderma is a result of the body producing too much collagen . . .

CHAPTER 4

Eyes

Let's play a little game, shall we? I spy with my little eye, something lumpy . . . and swollen . . . and crusty . . . and droopy . . . and goopy . . . and bloody. You know what? Maybe this game wasn't such a good idea after all. Even though your eyes might be the window to your soul, that's not the only thing they can put on display. In fact, these two little windows can also show symptoms of disease, illness, and perhaps even life-threatening conditions. Window-shopping has never seemed so . . . terrifying.

IF YOUR EYES . . .

. . . have blood between the cornea and the iris

You could have cancer of the eye, a blood vessel abnormality, or inflammation of the iris, but you most likely have a condition known as hyphema. Hyphema is caused by a trauma to the eye—though it can also be a result of surgery—and severe bleeding usually occurs within three to five days following the trauma. However, a small painless hyphema can appear in the white of the eye for no known reason; if they keep happening, check with your doctor. While smaller hyphemas are not usually visible, a large hyphema can make it appear as if the entire eye is filled with blood. Should you have a hyphema, you should seek medical attention immediately. Hyphema also has the tendency to make any person look pretty horrifying. The condition is particularly frightening when found in children, hillbillies, cyborgs, or any person wielding a blunt object who seems to walk faster than you can run.

Bloody Tears?

Haemolacria is a rare condition that actually causes a person to cry tears that are partly made up of blood. Sometimes the tears are lightly tinged with a red color, while other times it looks like your eyes are pouring out pure blood. Haemolacria is sometimes associated with other illnesses, such as tumors, lesions, or bacterial conjunctivitis, or it can be the result of a trauma. Other times, however, the condition is spontaneous. These spontaneous occurrences of haemolacria are more commonly found in women who are menstruating, and it is believed that hormones play a role in this event. And if by "hormones" doctors really mean "zombie infestation," chances are you'd have to agree completely.

... are sensitive to light

You may have what is known as photophobia. Though it may sound bad, photophobia is not actually a result of any disease.

Causes of photophobia include inflammation inside the eye, a corneal abrasion or ulcer, a migraine, and even adverse reaction to drugs like amphetamines, cocaine, cyclopentolate, phenylephrine, or even the pupil-dilating drugs used by your eye doctor. Photophobia may also be caused by meningitis, infection, glaucoma, or a chalazion (a small bump on the eyelid caused by a blocked oil gland). If you wear contact lenses, it is important to take proper care of them. In 2006, there was a major outbreak among contact users of a fungal eye infection known as fusarium, which, among other symptoms, led to photophobia. While the fungal infection was a result of inadequate conditions from the maker of a certain contact lens solution, those who did not clean their contact lenses properly were at a greater risk of having the infection. If this infection were to go untreated, it could damage the eye to the point where a corneal transplant was necessary. Wouldn't you rather have something cool like haemolacria?

. . . blink frequently

There can be many causes. Sometimes it's just a simple problem with your contact lens or a foreign object in your eye. But blinking too much can also be a sign of blepharospasm, an increased amount of involuntary blinking that can lead to spasms of the eyes. Blepharospasm, believed to be a disorder of the central nervous system, can even cause a person to become functionally blind because the eyes are not able to stay open long enough to see. Blinking too frequently can also be a sign of a stroke or hemifacial spasm, which consists of involuntary muscle twitches on only one side of a person's face. This is usually caused when a blood vessel

Blinking too frequently can also be a sign of a stroke . . .

compresses the seventh cranial nerve in the brain or it can be a symptom of magnesium deficiency, which can cause muscle spasms in any part of the body. Lastly, blinking frequently can be associated with dry eye syndrome, which is a chronic dryness because the tear film (which is composed of mucus, water, and fat) of the eye is either reduced in quality or quantity or there is evaporation of the tear film. Other causes of blinking too frequently include trying to look cute or trying to desperately communicate via Morse code.

... have dilated pupils for an extended period of time

You may have a disorder known as mydriasis where the pupil stays dilated, even if you are in broad daylight. One of the most common causes of mydriasis is drug use (such as anticholinergics, hallucinogens, and even antidepressants), but mydriasis can also be caused by a trauma to the eye, a carotid artery aneurysm, brain damage, botulism, Adie syndrome (a neurological disorder that features the pupil of one eye being larger than the other, also known as Holmes-Adie syndrome or Adie's pupil), acute angle-closure glaucoma, or it can be a withdrawal symptom of drugs such as morphine and heroin. In some cases, mydriasis has even been linked to sexual arousal. So the next time you notice someone making eyes at you from across the room, make sure you check out their pupils . . .

... blink infrequently

You may have cranial nerve palsy, myasthenia gravis, Parkinson's disease, or a side effect of a Botox injection. Cranial nerve palsy of the eye is partial or full paralysis involving the third, fourth, or sixth cranial nerves. This can result in difficulty moving the eye and symptoms such as head tilting, having eyes that are not pointed in the same direction, a loss of vision, double vision, a reduced perception of depth, dilated pupils that do not respond to light, and ptosis (a drooping eyelid). Cranial nerve palsy can be caused by diabetes, trauma to the head, aneurysms, tumors, and death of tissue (known as infarction). Parkinson's disease is a neurological disorder where both movement and coordination are impaired, and this can lead to a decrease in blinking along with facial paralysis and a lack of any facial expression. Blinking infrequently is also a widespread epidemic among the mannequin community, and, sadly, there is no cure.

. . . are losing their eyelashes or eyebrows

You may have madarosis, a loss of eyelashes or eyebrows as a result of trauma, alopecia areata (an autoimmune disease that damages hair follicles), or blepharitis, an inflammation of the eyelid caused by an allergic reaction, dermatitis, and even rosacea. Blepharitis causes a burning and itching sensation, and it can create pain, tearing, swelling, dry eye, stickiness, and a crusty eyelid or eyelashes. There is currently no cure for the condition, though there are treatments that will lessen the symptoms. You may also have trichotillomania, a compulsive disorder in which a person has an irresistible urge to repeatedly pull the hair from his or her body. Most often, it involves areas such as the scalp, eyebrows, and eyelashes. The cause of trichotillomania is not known, though other reasons for pulling your own hair out might include having teenagers, discussing politics, and having to deal with your coworkers on a daily basis.

. . . have a red lump on the edge of the eyelid

You may have a stye, an infection of the upper or lower eyelid. These resemble boils or pimples and are usually filled with pus.

A stye can be caused by blepharitis (see previous entry), but it is commonly caused by bacteria (such as *Staphylococcus*) that enters your eyelid. Other symptoms of a stye include tearing, swelling of the eyelid, and pain. Common ways to expose your eyelids to infection include using expired makeup, not washing your hands before putting your contacts in, leaving eye makeup on overnight, not disinfecting your contact lenses, not washing your hands, or just having poor overall hygiene. While most sties will go away within a week, to help treat the condition, do not squeeze the stye, avoid wearing eye makeup and contact lenses, apply a warm compress four to six times each day for fifteen minutes at a time, and wear an eyepatch—the eyepatch doesn't do much for the stye, but it sure helps everyone else around you get a good laugh.

. . . have yellow or orange growths on the upper or lower eyelids

You may have a skin condition known as xanthelasma palpebrarum. While these soft growths that occur away from the eyelashes do not itch or cause pain, they can be a cosmetic issue for many, and unfortunately, they do not go away (and will often continue to grow). If you have xanthelasma palpebrarum you either inherited them or you may have high cholesterol levels in your blood, and you might be at risk for having atherosclerosis, ischemic heart disease, or a heart attack. Women are affected with xanthelasma palpebrarum more than men, and, while it is rarely seen in the United States, the condition is rather common in Asia and in the Mediterranean. So if you see a large group of people with this condition, know that you're not in Kansas anymore . . .

If only one eye is swollen . . .

You may have an infectious disease common to Mexico, Central America, and South America known as Chagas disease. Humans can get the disease by being bitten by a triatomine bug that is infected with a parasite known as *Trypanosoma cruzi*. Triatomine bugs will come out at night and feed on humans, and if you are bitten by an infected bug, it will leave the parasite on your skin. If you scratch the bite, this will actually help the parasite enter the body, and once inside, it will begin to multiply and spread. Other ways that you might become infected by the parasite include eating meat that is uncooked and that has the feces of an infected bug on it, being around a pet that is infected, or receiving a blood transfusion from someone who is infected with the disease. There are two phases of Chagas disease: an acute phase and a chronic phase. During the acute phase, you might experience one swollen eye, a fever, a rash, swelling where the bug bit you, and you will feel generally unwell. Following the acute phase, symptoms may not appear until ten to twenty years later. The chronic phase of Chagas disease can lead to inflammation of the heart, an irregular heartbeat, cardiac arrest, congestive heart failure, difficulty swallowing, and abdominal pain. Time to stock up on bug spray—and stop ordering your meat rare.

. . . have a thick, yellow, green, or white discharge

You may have conjunctivitis. Other symptoms include burning, itchy eyes and redness in the inner eyelid or white part of the eye (hence the "pink" in "pinkeye"). Viruses, bacteria, irritants, and allergies can all cause conjunctivitis, which is an inflammation of the conjunctiva, a clear tissue that lines along the interior of the eyelid and over the white of your eye. When caused by a virus or bacteria, conjunctivitis is incredibly contagious. Though most forms of conjunctivitis are very easy to cure with the aid of eye drops or antibiotics, certain forms (such as conjunctivitis caused by chlamydia or gonorrhea) can lead to scarring of the cornea and conjunctivae (the mucous membranes that cover the white part of your eyes), and ultimately, blindness. So remember kids, have safe sex or go blind. I'd say that gets the point across . . .

. . . have chronic conjunctivitis

You may have a blocked tear duct, which can be caused by an injury to the eye, a tumor, an infection, inflammation, or getting older (where the openings in your upper and lower eyelids become more narrow). Some people are even born with the condition (where the tear drainage system has not fully formed). Symptoms of a blocked tear duct include recurrent conjunctivitis, recurrent eye infections, excessive tearing, bloody tears, having a mucous discharge, and experiencing blurred vision and watery eyes. Usually, a blocked tear duct can be corrected with a expanding probe, but treatment varies depending on the cause of the condition, your age, and whether you can stop crying for two seconds to have the surgery.

Conjunctivitis

. . . are drooping

You may have a neuromuscular disorder known as myasthenia gravis, which is responsible for weakening the voluntary muscles. Myasthenia gravis occurs when the immune system attacks healthy tissue, and communication between the muscles and nerves is broken down. Myasthenia gravis commonly occurs in women under the age of forty and men over the age of sixty. A drooping eyelid or having double vision are the first symptoms to appear in more than half of the people who are diagnosed with this disorder. While the neck, legs, and arms are weakened from myasthenia gravis, you may also experience muscle weakness in your eyes, throat, or face. Other symptoms of the disorder include difficulty swallowing, having less control in making facial expressions, having an altered speech, not being able to hold your head up, and waddling while walking. In other words, you'll look like your drunk uncle on Thanksgiving.

You may also experience muscle weakness in your eyes, throat, or face.

You may be able to see more from your eyes than you thought possible . . .

According to the teachings of ayurvedic medicine, your eyes can actually be indicators of certain conditions. Having a yellow conjunctiva might mean you have a weak liver. If your iris is small, this can be a sign that you have weak joints. If your eyes are prominent (where the eyelids are full and extend from your face), this could mean you have thyroid gland dysfunction. If a white ring is present around the iris, this could mean you have too much sugar or salt in your diet. If this white ring is very white in color and prominent, this can be a sign of joint degeneration and could potentially lead to joint pain and arthritis. If your eyes are closed, this can lead to the inability to see, a tendency to bump into objects, and the risk of falling asleep.

CHAPTER 5

Ears

Sometimes, finally understanding what's wrong with you can sound like music to your ears. That is, of course, assuming you still can hear . . . or that your ears aren't ringing . . . or full of blisters . . . or oozing a yellow pus. Whether you've spent too long in the swimming pool or your ear is becoming deformed, this chapter has the answer to all of your symptoms. So listen carefully, because you definitely don't want to turn a deaf ear to the info found here (although, you may have no choice in the matter).

IF YOUR EAR(S) . . .

. . . hurt

You most likely have otitis media, a.k.a. an ear infection. When you have otitis media, your middle ear (the part of the ear located behind the eardrum) is infected and inflamed. This, the most common type of ear infection, is a result of the eustachian tube (which normally clears any mucus from the middle ear) becoming blocked, leading to a buildup of fluid. Ear infections are most common with babies because their eustachian tubes are more horizontal, narrower, and shorter, so they easily clog. An ear infection may occur following a cold or the flu, and beyond ear pain, other symptoms include vomiting, diarrhea, and hearing loss in the infected ear. Should your ear start to suddenly drain a yellow or green fluid, you may have a ruptured eardrum. On the bright side, between the vomiting, the diarrhea, and the yellowy fluid coming out of your ear, you won't even be able to tell that your ear hurts.

Ear infections are most common with babies because their eustachian tubes are more horizontal, narrower, and shorter, so they easily clog.

. . . are red on the outside

You might be experiencing otitis externa, otherwise known to anyone who has lifeguarded as swimmer's ear. Unlike otitis media, which is an infection of the middle ear, swimmer's ear is an infection of the outer ear canal (the part of the ear that you can see). Oftentimes, swimmer's ear is caused by water that remains in the ear. The moisture breaks the skin lining (which acts as a barrier to protect you from infection), which allows for the growth of bacteria. The pain from swimmer's ear begins within a day or two, and other symptoms include swelling of the ear and a yellow, white, clear, or bloody drainage. Sounds like something you'd see on *Baywatch*, right?

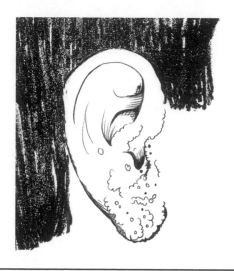

Swimmer's ear

. . . are ringing and you feel plugged up

Your outer ear canal may be blocked by something known as cerumen impaction. In other words, you've got earwax—and a lot of it. Cerumen, or earwax, is produced in the outer ear canal as a way to stop dirt, water, fungus, and bacteria from entering the inner ear, and it also gets rid of dead skin cells. If your earwax dries up and starts to accumulate, it can actually get stuck in the ear canal. This can lead to trouble hearing, itchiness or pain, and dizziness. Some skin diseases, like keratosis obturans, actually make you produce too much earwax. If the earwax is not removed, your symptoms will worsen and you also can get an infection and irritation. What's worse, removing the earwax can also lead to infection and bleeding, and if the eardrum is injured, it can cause deafness. Other causes of cerumen impaction include wearing a hearing aid, incorrectly using cotton swabs, and getting older (as you age, your earwax gets drier). Cerumen impaction is most common in those with mental health problems, men, and the elderly. You would think that with all of that ear hair, older men would have figured out a way around this earwax problem . . .

. . . have lost hearing on one side

It might be a sign of acoustic neuroma or neurofibromatosis, a noncancerous tumor that presses on the nerve that connects the ear and the brain. Although symptoms may be mild or not present in the beginning, as the tumor grows, the symptoms will become much more evident. These symptoms include a loss of balance, vertigo, facial weakness and numbness, and tinnitus (ringing in the ears). Neurofibromatosis is a genetic disorder where tumors affect the hearing nerves on both sides. Should the tumor grow large enough, it can become life threatening and begin to press against the brain. It has been noted that people with neurofibromatosis have often referred to people with acoustic neuroma as "wussies." Too bad the acoustic neuroma sufferers didn't hear the insult . . .

> As the tumor grows, the symptoms will become much more evident.

. . . has a painful rash with fluid-filled blisters

You may have Ramsay Hunt syndrome, which is actually the result of shingles (see the entry on shingles in Chapter 9). If this infection affects the facial nerve near your ear, it can lead to facial paralysis and hearing loss of that ear, and this painful rash in and around the entrance to the ear canal will develop at around the same time the facial paralysis begins. Any person who has had the chickenpox can get Ramsay Hunt syndrome (because shingles is caused by the same virus that causes chickenpox); however, Ramsay Hunt syndrome rarely occurs in children and is mostly seen in people sixty years old or older. While the loss of hearing and facial paralysis associated with Ramsay Hunt syndrome is usually temporary, it can become permanent. The facial weakness this syndrome causes can also make closing the eyelid difficult, which can in turn damage the clear tissue that is over your cornea. It's not all bad though: the temporary paralysis associated with Ramsay Hunt syndrome is kind of like taking a snapshot of your face. The downside, of course, is you'll most likely be frozen with a look of "What the hell are these blisters on my ear?"

... stick out due to a swelling behind them

You may have mastoiditis, an infection of the mastoid bone found in the skull. Generally, mastoiditis is caused by a middle ear infection that has spread to the mastoid bone from the middle ear. The mastoid bone, which is normally a honeycomb-like shape, begins to fill with infected material and can start to deteriorate. Other symptoms of mastoiditis include drainage coming out of the ear, redness behind the ear, redness of the ear, swelling, a loss of hearing, a fever that suddenly increases, and headaches. At one point in time, before antibiotics were around, mastoiditis was one of the leading causes of death for children. Today, it is less common and less dangerous; however, it can recur following treatment. So just remember, if your ears stick out, take notice (I'm sure everyone else has).

... is swollen or deformed

You may have an infection known as perichondritis, an infection of the cartilage around the outer ear that is mainly caused by a bacterium known as *Pseudomonas aeruginosis*. Usually, the skin infection is a result of a trauma, such as an injury from contact sports or ear surgery, but the most common cause of perichondritis today is from having the cartilage pierced. Perichondritis can lead to chondritis, a very serious condition where the cartilage becomes infected and the structure of the ear becomes damaged. Symptoms of perichondritis include pain, swelling, and redness, and in more severe cases, the structure of the ear can become deformed, the person can suffer from a fever, and there can be a fluid discharge or pus. To treat perichondritis, you will need to take antibiotics, and if the infection is severe, surgery to remove some parts of the ear may be required. But you can always cover up that deformed spot with a big old earring!

That sounds tasty . . .

Some people experience a rare condition known as synesthesia, where the senses are actually joined or bleed into one another. For example, listening to music or looking at letters can make a person with synesthesia see colors. In one rare type of synesthesia, known as lexical-gustatory synesthesia, when a person hears a word or sound, he or she can actually taste it. And we're not talking about just food words. A study in 2006 showed that people with lexical-gustatory synesthesia have specific tastes for common, everyday words, and that the sound of the word and rhyming play a part in how the word tastes. For example, it was noted that when people in the study heard the word "Tony," they tasted macaroni, and when they heard words with an "a" sound in it, it tasted like bacon. Let's just hope they don't often hear words ending in "oop."

CHAPTER 6

Nose

There's nothing worse than a runny, bumpy, or red nose when all you want to do is be able to breathe properly and know what the hell is going on! In this chapter, you'll finally learn what's going on in that schnoz of yours—even if the outcome doesn't look (or smell) all that good. From sinus infections and nasal polyps to von Willebrand disease and nasal cavity cancer, or even a bad case of allergies, always remember to do as the great Toucan Sam would and "follow your nose." In the end, you might finally be able to stop and smell the roses—unless, of course, you're allergic to them . . .

IF YOUR NOSE . . .

. . . feels congested and obstructed

You may have nasal polyps, noncancerous growths the shape of a teardrop that can form in the sinuses or nose. Unlike the polyps found in the bladder or colon, nasal polyps rarely become malignant, and if they are small enough, no symptoms will occur and treatment is not necessary. However, if a nasal polyp becomes large enough, it can block the drainage from your sinuses, and if too much mucus accumulates in your sinuses, you risk getting frequent infections, breathing problems, and hyposmia (a loss of smell). Other symptoms include postnasal drip, facial pain, a runny nose, sneezing, anosmia (loss of smell), and itchiness around the eyes. Nasal polyps may also be caused by food allergies. Surgery and medication are used to treat nasal polyps, but after treatment, they often return. Just think of your nasal polyps as that annoying little brother who always used to bug you and your friends. Sure, you can shake him off for a little bit, but he can only be distracted for so long until he comes right back.

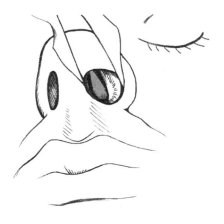

Nasal polyp

... is congested and you frequently have sinus infections

This could be a sign of a deviated septum, a condition where the nasal septum (the cartilage and bone responsible for dividing the nasal cavity) is crooked or off center. A deviated septum can be caused by a trauma or injury to the nose, and some people are actually born with it. Symptoms of the condition include postnasal drip, headaches, nosebleeds, facial pain, and perhaps the most annoying symptom for your spouse, loud snoring while you sleep. Having a deviated septum can lead to serious breathing problems such as sleep apnea, where a person actually stops breathing for 10 seconds or longer while asleep. To fix a deviated septum, you must undergo a surgical procedure known as a septoplasty, in which a small incision is made in the septum and the excess bone or cartilage is removed. If you have the surgery, you'll be in good company. Celebrities like Ashlee Simpson, Barry Manilow, and Jennifer Aniston also underwent this procedure to correct a "deviated septum." Sure they did . . .

The most annoying symptom for your spouse is the loud snoring while you sleep.

. . . is swollen or crooked

I hope the other guy looks worse, because you may have a broken nose. Symptoms of a broken nose can appear instantly or can take up to three days to start showing. Other symptoms of a broken nose include bruising around the eyes, difficulty breathing, discharge of mucus, and bleeding from the nose. Broken noses are usually the result of a trauma, and 34 percent of all broken noses in 2009 were a result of fighting. A broken nose can lead to a deviated septum, a fracture of the cartilage, or a septal hematoma, which is when blood collects and blocks one or both of your nostrils. So next time, keep your fists up, your head down, and your legs pointed toward the nearest way out.

Your nose has personality . . .

According to ayurvedic medicine, every person is made up of a combination of three energies, known as doshas, that determine our emotional, mental, and physical characteristics, and usually one or two of these doshas are more dominant. When we have an imbalance of our doshas, the result is illness. People who believe in ayurveda believe that the nose can actually determine which dosha is dominant in a person. In ayurvedic practice, someone with a crooked nose has a Vata dosha (these people talk a lot, move a lot, worry a lot, and are very creative), someone with a blunt nose has a Kapha dosha (these people are nurturers, listeners, and always happy), and someone with a sharp nose has a Pitta dosha (these people are sharp, witty, fiery, and make good leaders). If you have a hook nose, this means you are able to catch more fish when your head is underwater.

. . . has a bad smelling, thick green or yellow mucus

You probably have sinusitis, otherwise known as a sinus infection. A sinus infection occurs when your sinuses, which are normally full of air, become swollen. This swelling blocks the sinus exits and they begin to fill up with mucus. The accumulation of mucus provides the perfect home for bacteria to grow and, ultimately, cause an infection. In many cases, a sinus infection starts out from the common cold, which creates the inflammation of the sinuses to begin with. A person suffering from a sinus infection may experience a pressure or pain around the eyes and face, a fever, a cold that does not seem to go away, congestion, and a headache in the forehead. Though you may think you just have a cold, if you are experiencing pain in your face and have a thick nasal discharge for longer than a week, it very well could be a sinus infection. No word on how you're supposed to smell your mucus if your nose is blocked, but if yours seems funky, get it checked!

... is congested and you have swelling in the neck or face

You may have a type of cancer known as nasal cavity cancer. This cancer forms from the cells that line the inside of your nose that are responsible for producing mucus. Nasal cavity cancer is more common in men and in people who work around wood, leather, textiles, asbestos, metal plating, and flour. Symptoms of nasal cavity cancer are very similar to other conditions like a sinus infection or cold, and as a result, it can easily go unnoticed in the beginning. Other symptoms include nasal pain, fatigue, loss of smell, problems hearing and speaking, problems breathing, a lump in the nose, headaches, and pain and nerve issues as the cancer spreads. The good thing about nasal cavity cancer, however, is that it can be detected earlier than other sinus cancers due to the fact that it blocks the nose. If the cancer reaches the lymph nodes, your neck and face may swell, though this is usually painless. There is good news, though. Nasal cavity cancer is very rare, and only about 1,000 people a year are diagnosed with it

> Nasal cavity cancer can be detected earlier than other sinus cancers . . .

in the United States; they're the ones who didn't wear masks when clearing that asbestos out of your house.

... is runny, itchy, and congested and you have a decreased sense of smell and taste

You may have hay fever, or allergic rhinitis. Hay fever feels very much like a cold, only it is not caused by a virus but rather an allergic reaction. One out of five people are affected by hay fever, and common causes include pollen, molds, fungi, cockroaches (yes, for some people cockroaches are more than just a nuisance—they're an allergy), dust mites, and pet dander. Other symptoms of hay fever include eyes that itch or are watery, sneezing, coughing, blue and swollen skin under your eyes, and facial pain and sinus pressure. Depending on what you are allergic to, you may react during certain times of the year (tree pollen, for example, is common in the springtime), or you may react year-round (like with cockroaches—including their feces, saliva, and bodies). To tell whether you have hay fever or just a cold, take a good look at your symptoms. If your symptoms last for days, you probably have a cold. If your symptoms seem to appear only when exposed to a certain environment, you probably have hay fever. If you can't tell because you have roaches all over your apartment, get rid of the damn roaches! Did you actually need to hear that before you did something?

> **How's this for misleading?**
> Hay fever is almost never caused by hay. Oh, and the condition doesn't cause a fever. It makes so much sense now!

... has recurrent and extended nosebleeds

This can be a sign of von Willebrand disease (vWD), the most common inherited bleeding disorder, which occurs as a result of an impairment or deficiency of the von Willebrand factor, a protein in the blood that is essential for blood clotting. When a person with von Willebrand disease gets a cut, his or her body takes a much longer time to form a clot and stop the bleeding. Symptoms of von Willebrand disease can be subtle or extreme, depending on the person. In fact, some people do not even realize they have the disorder until they have had surgery or a serious trauma that results in excessive bleeding. Some visible symptoms of von Willebrand disease include bleeding gums, bleeding from shaving, excessive bleeding from cuts or dental procedures like tooth extraction, blood in your urine or stool, easy bruising, or an increase in menstrual flow. If this sounds like you, we advise that you paint your walls red so you don't freak other people out when you pick at a hangnail.

CHAPTER 7

Mouth

As a frequent patient, you're by now used to opening your mouth and saying "ah." And as a hypochondriac, you're no doubt used to opening your mouth and screaming "aaahhhh!" In this chapter, you'll learn all the reasons why you should combine the two! Depending on your symptoms, you might never get past that initial scream of horror. But at least you'll have some information to chew on while you panic.

IF YOUR MOUTH . . .

. . . has a blister or lesion

You may have a cold sore. Cold sores are actually found on the lips and are caused by herpes simplex virus type 1 (and out of the two types of herpes simplex, it's a safe bet to say this is the one you'd want). These small and painful blisters can last around the lip area for ten to fourteen days, and while there is no cure, there are a ton of ointments and home remedies that can help alleviate the symptoms. Fun fact: More than half of the

United States population is infected with type 1 herpes virus by the time they are in their twenties. Not so fun fact: *More than half of the United States population is infected with type 1 herpes virus by the time they are in their twenties*. No one is safe.

... has several blisters

You may have an autoimmune disorder known as pemphigus. Pemphigus is actually a term for a rare group of disorders that result in blisters most commonly found in the mouth and on the genitals. Often, people who are middle-aged or older are affected, and pemphigus vulgaris, the most common type of these disorders, is more prevalent in people of Jewish and Middle Eastern descent. The main types of pemphigus are pemphigus vulgaris (which features painful blisters in the mouth or genitals that erupt and ooze), pemphigus foliaceus (which features itchy, but not painful, blisters on the scalp, head, and later the back and chest), paraneoplastic pemphigus (which features painful sores on the mouth and esophagus, is associated with different types of cancer, and can lead to progressive lung disease), and pemphigus scareseveryonearoundyou (which features blisters that scare the crap out of everyone around you).

Pemphigus is ... a term for a rare group of disorders ...

... cracks at the corners

You may have a chronic inflammatory condition known as angular cheilitis. Usually, angular cheilitis, which is related to another condition known simply as cheilitis (or more commonly, chapped lips), is caused by a fungal or bacterial infection and is the result of saliva accumulation that occurs in the corner of the mouth. Symptoms of angular cheilitis include slight pain, redness, cracking of the skin, ulceration, and a drainage of pus. If treated properly, angular cheilitis can go away within days; however, the condition can last for months if not treated. People who suffer from angular cheilitis may also have a vitamin B_{12} deficiency, an iron deficiency, or a folate deficiency, and those who have diabetes mellitus or have undergone radiation in the head or neck are more prone to having the condition. For some people, it turns out that "mouth-watering" isn't always a good thing . . .

. . . has a small ulcer or sore that is white, round, and has a red border

You may have a canker sore. The good news is that, unlike cold sores, a virus does not cause canker sores. The bad news is no one really knows what actually does cause them. Whereas cold sores can occur on the lips, under the chin, and even under the nose, canker sores only occur inside the mouth. Canker sores can be broken down into two types: simple and complex. Simple canker sores often occur in people age ten to twenty, occur three to four times a year, and last for about a week. Complex canker sores, which are less common, occur more often in people with a history of having canker sores and can be a sign of an underlying health issue such as an impaired immune system, bad dental alignment leading to biting the inside of your mouth, bioflavonoid deficiency, iron deficiency, or gastrointestinal tract disease. But don't be fooled—whether your canker sore is simple or complex, it's going to hurt all the same.

. . . has white patches inside and on your tongue

You may have a yeast infection known as thrush. Besides sounding like the name of a punk rock band, thrush is caused by candida, a fungus that is normally present in the mouth. When you have a weaker immune system, your body is not able to keep candida in check with enough good bacteria, and the fungus begins to grow. Underneath the white patches, you might have red tissue that bleeds easily, and the sores can increase in size and number. Thrush often occurs in babies who can develop it during their trip down the birth canal if their mother had a vaginal yeast infection. Taking antibiotics, eating yogurt, rinsing with a hydrogen peroxide solution, and using antifungal mouthwash can all be used to treat thrush. In babies, treatment may not even be necessary, and often the infection will go away in just two weeks. Nothing passes the time quite like sitting around waiting for the white fuzz on your tongue to go away . . .

. . . has white, thick patches that cannot be wiped away

You may have something known as leukoplakia. Leukoplakia is usually found on the tongue, gums, inside of the cheeks, and bottom of the mouth, and in most cases it is caused by the use of tobacco (both smoking and chewing tobacco). It's even been reported that three out of four people who use smokeless tobacco products will eventually develop the condition in the part of their mouth where they hold the tobacco. People with weakened immune systems due to conditions like HIV or AIDS can actually develop a type of leukoplakia known as hairy leukoplakia, which causes white, fuzzy patches along the sides of the tongue. Though most cases of leukoplakia are benign, some

> Leukoplakia . . . is caused by the use of tobacco.

cases can actually be a sign of cancer of the mouth that will often appear next to areas of leukoplakia. If you needed another reason to never use tobacco, think about how sexy you will be when your tongue looks like cowhide . . .

. . . clicks when you open it or chew

You may have a temporomandibular joint disorder, or TMJ disorder. The temporomandibular joint, which is where the lower jawbone meets the upper jawbone, is the joint that allows you to chew, talk, and yawn. TMJ disorders can be due to several things, including muscle fatigue from grinding your teeth or clenching, jaw injury, overly aggressive dental work, and arthritis. Other symptoms include pain in the jaw, difficulty opening and closing the mouth due to the jaw locking, having pain in or around the ear, having difficulty chewing, and having an uneven bite. If your jaw clicks and you aren't experiencing pain, you most likely do not have a TMJ disorder. TMJ disorders are more common in women from the ages of thirty to fifty, and they often occur more in people who have sleep disorders, fibromyalgia, rheumatoid arthritis, or chronic fatigue syndrome. If the clicking becomes too unbearable for the people around you, you might have more success living with the bushmen of Africa where clicks are a staple of their dialect.

. . . has lumps, bumps, bleeding, and you get constant sores that don't go away

You may have oral cancer. If not diagnosed and treated early on, this can be fatal. According to the American Cancer Society, men over the age of fifty are at the greatest risk when it comes to getting oral cancer, and use of tobacco greatly enhances this risk. Pipe, cigar, and cigarette smokers are six times more likely to develop oral cancer than nonsmokers, and users of smoke-less tobacco products are fifty times more likely. Drinking alcohol and sun-damaged lips also make a person more vulnerable, as well as a family history of cancer. Only 25 percent of patients diagnosed with oral cancer are nonsmokers. Other symptoms of oral cancer include crusts or eroded areas inside the mouth or on the lips and gums, red or white (or a combination of red and white) patches inside the mouth, a change in voice and hoarseness, and weight loss. Sounds like you need to lay off the smoking if you want to remain smoking hot.

... has swollen, puffy, receding, or tender gums

You may have gingivitis. Rarely is gingivitis painful . . . to you. However, since one of the common symptoms of gingivitis is bad breath, to other people gingivitis can be menacing. Gingivitis is actually a mild form of gum disease (so mild that you may not be aware that you have it), and other symptoms include gums that will bleed after flossing or brushing, and red gums instead of pink gums. Gingivitis is most commonly caused by poor oral hygiene, and daily brushing of your teeth and flossing are your best ways to prevent it. If not cared for, gingivitis can lead to tooth loss, more serious cases of gum disease, a nonexistent social life, and the ability to knock a person down from across the room without ever touching them.

... has swollen, bright red or purple gums, and you have pus coming out of your gums

You did not take your dentist seriously when he told you to fix your gingivitis, and now you may have periodontitis. This is a gum infection that is quite serious and will destroy the bone and soft tissue supporting your teeth. Not only does periodontitis lead to tooth loss, but it even increases your risk of heart attack and stroke. Other symptoms include bad breath, receding and tender gums, loose teeth, a bad taste left in your mouth, and spaces that actually develop between the teeth. Once you have an advanced level of periodontitis, maintaining a good level of oral hygiene will not be enough to treat the condition, and your only options will be to undergo surgeries like bone grafting, soft tissue grafts, and flap surgery. If your periodontitis has not advanced too much, nonsurgical options include ozone treatments with your water pic, scaling (removing the tartar), root planing (smoothing the surface of the root), taking antibiotics and probiotics, and wearing a paper bag on your head.

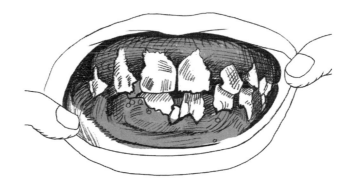

Periodontitis

. . . has bad breath

This can be a sign of a number of problems and conditions. While you already know how certain gum infections can make your mouth smell like the inside of a dumpster, bad breath can also be the result of tooth decay, cavities, an abscessed tooth, dry mouth, thrush, and even certain cancers. Leukemia, oral tumors, and stomach, esophageal, and throat cancers can all result in bad breath due to the fact that there is decay in the body, and treatment can actually worsen the smell. Of course, bad breath can also be a result of your diet. Foods that are high in protein, like meat, fish, eggs, cheese, and other dairy products, will usually lead to bad breath. So lay off the fish sticks and milk come lunch time . . .

Alcohol under the breath

If you or someone you know always has breath that smells of alcohol, and in particular like nail polish remover, this is a sign of diabetes. The main ingredient of nail polish remover is acetone, and this is actually found naturally in the body. If you do not have enough insulin in your body or your body is not able to use the insulin, instead of using glucose for energy, your body will use fat, and this process causes levels of acetone to rise. For this reason, many diabetics give off an odor that is like a fruity gum or like nail polish remover. Of course, sometimes alcohol under the breath really is just from drinking alcohol. So make sure you know all of the facts before you start injecting someone with insulin . . .

. . . has jaw spasms

It looks like you might not have gotten all of your shots. Jaw spasms are the beginning signs of tetanus (or lockjaw), a disease of the nervous system that can be fatal. Tetanus is caused by *Clostridium tetani*, a bacteria found in animal feces, dust, and soil. The bacteria that causes tetanus only thrives in an environment that lacks oxygen—and a deep wound in your body is the perfect living space. People with tetanus have extremely painful spasms of the jaw and neck, and these spasms can create respiratory failure, provoke cardiac arrest, and can ultimately lead to death. Other symptoms of tetanus include difficulty swallowing, neck and abdominal muscle stiffness, and body spasms, usually triggered by minor things such as light breezes, touches, or loud sounds, which can last for minutes. So if you're not up on your shots, you may want to avoid throwing your hat into that knife fight.

> A deep wound ... is the perfect living space.

... has a pale ring around it

You may have scarlet fever. The same bacteria that cause strep throat also cause scarlet fever. The symptoms of scarlet fever include a rash that appears as if it is a sunburn but feels like sandpaper (this rash starts at the neck or face and moves down the body to the arms and legs), deep red lines at the folds of the body (such as the armpits, knees, groin, elbows, and neck), a flushed face that features a pale ring that goes around the mouth, and a tongue that is red, bumpy, and looks like a strawberry. The strawberry tongue and rash only last for about a week and are followed by the peeling of the affected skin, a very sore throat, nausea, vomiting, headaches, enlarged lymph nodes in the neck, and a fever of 101°F. Children between the ages of five and fifteen are most likely to develop scarlet fever, which, if not treated with antibiotics, can eventually affect the nervous system and the heart. Who knew a strawberry tongue could be so sour?

Speaking of tongue colors . . .

According to ayurvedic medicine, opening your mouth is kind of like opening a box of crayons. Just as each of those crayons has a specific name for every color, so does your tongue! Only instead of funny names, it's illnesses! A tongue that is pale means that you are lacking blood in your body or that you are anemic. A tongue that is yellowish in color means that you might have liver disease or excess bile in your gallbladder. A tongue that is blue in color usually means you have a problem with your heart. A tongue that is whitish in color means you have mucus accumulation and an imbalance of your Kapha (the energy responsible for controlling growth by maintaining your immune system, moisturizing your skin, and supplying water to your body). A tongue that is green or red signifies an imbalance of your Pitta (the energy responsible for controlling your body's metabolic system, including absorption, digestion, the temperature of your body, and your nutrition). A tongue that is black or brown means you have an imbalance in your Vata (the energy that controls motion, your heartbeat, circulation of the blood, breathing, and blinking). And a tongue that is orange means you have an imbalance in your variety of beverages—and you should probably lay off the Sunkist for a while.

. . . has a black, hairy tongue

There is no need to panic. Even though it looks like you have a small dog inside of your mouth, a black, hairy tongue is completely harmless. When the raised protrusions of the tongue (known as papillae) elongate and do not shed as normally as they should, the tongue starts to take on a hairy appearance. Bacteria, debris, and other organisms begin to collect on the papillae, giving the tongue a black, brown, or yellowish color. Black, hairy tongue is typically caused by an overgrowth of bacteria or yeast in the mouth and will usually go away on its own. Other potential causes of this condition include poor oral hygiene, breathing through the mouth, heavy use of tobacco products, and taking medications that contain bismuth, the active ingredient in Pepto-Bismol. Other symptoms of black, hairy tongue include having an altered sense of taste, having a metallic taste in your mouth, and having bad breath. Though, considering you have the equivalent of a wet dog on your tongue, bad breath shouldn't really come as much of a surprise.

CHAPTER 8

Neck

Does your neck suddenly look like it belongs to a football player? Is your Adam's apple fighting for space with a lump and losing? Is the fact that your lymph nodes are the size of chicken eggs making you a little cuckoo? You're not just being a pain in the neck; you have symptoms that need to be diagnosed and dealt with. So if you ever want to walk around in public without a scarf on, you'd better start reading. Not only will you finally be able to close that top button on your shirt, but you might just save your life.

IF YOUR NECK . . .

. . . is swollen

Your lymph nodes are probably inflamed. The lymph nodes play a crucial role in fighting off viruses, bacteria, and illness in the body. The lymph nodes will become swollen when exposed to a virus or bacteria, and the most common reason for swollen lymph nodes is from an infection (especially viral infections).

Common infections that lead to swelling of the lymph nodes (also known as lymphadenitis) include the viruses: the common cold, measles, and mononucleosis (otherwise known as the kissing disease). The bacteria include strep throat, the measles, and an infected tooth. Should you have swollen lymph nodes accompanied by a sore throat, difficulty swallowing or breathing, a persistent fever, night sweats, or if the swelling continues/remains the same for longer than two weeks, feels rubbery or hard, and does not move when pushed on, seek medical attention. Hardening of the swollen area might indicate a tumor, which doesn't sound as much fun as the kissing disease.

... is itching, blistering, burning, bleeding, or peeling

You may have a neck rash. This inflammatory reaction can make your neck appear red, white, purple, and even silver in color, and feel bumpy or flat. Most of the time, neck rashes are caused by acne, dermatitis, inflammatory disorders, contact dermatitis, and allergic reactions. Neck rashes can also lead to scaling and flaking of dead skin and can appear as one large rash or as small dots. While most neck rashes do not create permanent harm and go away in time, a neck rash can be a sign of an underlying illness, like meningitis, shingles, or a bacterial infection. Other symptoms may include flulike symptoms, red eyes, sneezing, a runny nose, and vomiting. Neck rashes are kind of like your body's way of giving itself a hickey ... so pull out that turtleneck if you feel one coming on.

A neck rash can be a sign of an underlying illness ...

. . . is twisted

You may have what is known as torticollis. This involves a twisting of the neck muscles beyond what is normal, leaving a person's head tipped to one side and the chin turned to the other side, or even the inability to turn the head to one side. Torticollis can occur as a result of a trauma, can be an adverse reaction from a medication, and can even run in the family (this is known as spasmodic torticollis). To treat the condition, your options include taking magnesium, stretching, physical devices such as braces, anti-spasmodic medication, Botox (or as the professionals call it: botulinum toxin), and, rarely, surgery. Torticollis can also make any person seem condescending and make any comment instantly sarcastic. Woman: Do you want to take this relationship to the next level? Man with torticollis: Yeah. That sounds like a great idea. I'd love that. Woman: You're such a jerk!

. . . has a lump

You may have thyroid cancer. The thyroid, which is responsible for producing hormones that regulate the body's weight, blood pressure, heart rate, and body temperature, is a butterfly-shaped gland found at the base of the neck. As the cancer begins to grow, signs and symptoms appear. Besides a lump in your neck, other symptoms of thyroid cancer include an increasingly hoarse voice, difficulty swallowing, and swollen lymph nodes. There are several different types of thyroid cancer, including papillary thyroid cancer (which is most common), follicular thyroid cancer, anaplastic thyroid cancer, and

As the cancer begins to grow, signs and symptoms appear.

thyroid lymphoma. If you had thyroid cancer and your thyroid was removed, you still risk having the disease return (due to microscopic cancer cells that have spread elsewhere), and the cancer can even reappear decades after treatment. The good news is that this cancer is slow growing and you can keep having it treated, making the survival rate 95 percent over 30 to 40 years. So the next time you tell someone you have a lump in your throat, it doesn't necessarily mean you're sad—you could just have a swollen butterfly-shaped gland that no longer functions properly.

> ### In case you thought living near a nuclear power plant was a good idea . . .
>
> Shockingly, you were wrong. An accident at a nuclear power plant can lead to thyroid cancer, and in the United States, anyone living within ten miles of a nuclear power plant may be eligible for potassium iodide tablets, which are used to block radiation from the thyroid and help prevent thyroid cancer. Sure, the rent near a nuclear power plant may be cheap, but if your favorite Sunday morning activity is sitting down to watch your three-eyed neighbor walking his Cyclops dog while his son plays catch with his own tentacles, it might be a sign that you should break your lease.

. . . swells at the base

You may have a goiter. A goiter occurs when the thyroid gland grows larger than normal. Though it can be a sign of thyroid cancer, that's not necessarily the cause, and if the goiter is small enough, it can go untreated. Goiters usually do not hurt, though if it becomes too large, you can have difficulty breathing or swallowing, and it can lead to a cough. There are many reasons why a person might develop a goiter, but the most common cause is an iodine deficiency, or in layman's terms, lacking iodine in your diet. Other reasons why you might develop a goiter include Graves' disease (where your thyroid gland swells due to inflammation and an autoimmune reaction), Hashimoto's disease (where your thyroid gland produces too few hormones and hormones from the pituitary gland push the thyroid to work harder), and even pregnancy. So the next time you're at the dinner table, pass the iodine-infused salt and keep it coming. What's a little high blood pressure if you don't have to live the rest of your life wearing a scarf.

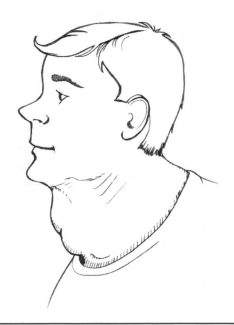

Goiter

. . . has swollen lymph nodes the size of a chicken egg

You may have the bubonic plague, or as it was called in medieval Europe, the Black Death (isn't that comforting?). The organism responsible for the plague is known as *Yersinia pestis*, and it is found in a type of small rodent that can be seen on every continent except Australia. People contract the illness via fleas that come from infected rats, rabbits, squirrels, chipmunks, prairie dogs, and even cats. There are three types of plague depending on which part of the body is affected: bubonic (the most common form that features swollen lymph nodes of the neck, groin, and armpit), septicemic (which features bleeding from the rectum, mouth, and under the skin and gangrene in the limbs and extremities), and pneumonic (which affects the lungs and features a cough with saliva and mucus that is bloody). Luckily for you, the outcome of having the plague is not so . . . well . . . black. If you have the plague, you will be put into isolation and given very strong antibiotics. But why take the chance? The next time you hear from me, I'll be putting some shrimp on the barbie . . .

> People contract the illness via fleas that come from infected rats, rabbits, squirrels, chipmunks, prairie dogs, and even cats.

If you have a stiff neck and fever . . .

You may have meningitis. Meningitis involves an inflammation of the meninges, membranes that surround the brain and spinal cord. Usually meningitis is the result of a viral infection and will go away on its own within two weeks. If caused by a bacterial infection, however, the condition can become life threatening. The most telltale signs of meningitis include having a stiff neck with flulike symptoms (and for this reason, it is common to mistake your symptoms for something less serious). In order to treat the condition properly, learning the source of the infection via a spinal tap is crucial because meningitis caused by particular bacteria are treated differently from meningitis caused by a virus, fungus, or even other types of bacteria. If untreated, meningitis can cause seizures, blindness, hearing loss, paralysis, learning disabilities, memory problems, a loss of the ability to speak, kidney failure, brain damage, and, ultimately, death. Find the cause of your stiff neck or end up a stiff.

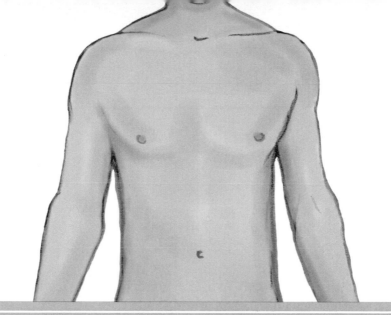

Part 2

The Torso

Skin • Shoulders • Back • Arms • Hands • Fingers • Chest • Breasts • Stomach • Pelvis • Buttocks

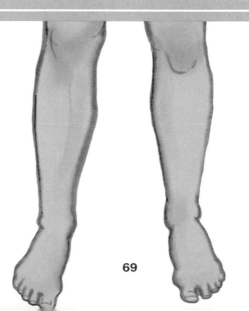

CHAPTER 9

Skin

What's the skinny on your skin? Do you have moles? Has a new rash emerged? Is your skin changing colors? Do you have spots or bumps? Are you developing a horn? Are you literally thick- or thin-skinned? The way your skin looks can tell a lot about you (and a lot about how people will look at you). But the best, or worst, part about your skin is that it's everywhere! Think of the diagnosing possibilities! Think of the countless hours you can now spend wondering which part of your body will kill you first! Why pay a dermatologist to do what you can do right in the comfort of your own germ-free and disinfected home? And you don't even need to schedule an appointment.

IF YOU HAVE A MOLE . . .

. . . that is asymmetrical, has different colors, has a border that is not well-defined, and has a diameter larger than an eraser at the end of a pencil

You should seek medical attention immediately, because this is most likely a form of skin cancer known as melanoma. Another clear sign of melanoma is a mole that seems to be changing in color, shape, and size. Now, don't panic just yet. It is entirely possible that you may simply have what is known as an atypical mole, which can look like melanoma but isn't. Often, atypical moles are larger than pencil erasers, have strange shapes, and are more than one color. If, however, you have four atypical moles or a parent, sibling, or child who has had melanoma, or if you have previously had melanoma, you are at greater risk for having melanoma. However, if that brown spot on your arm rubs away with saliva, that's the chocolate pudding you ate at lunch. And you're a slob.

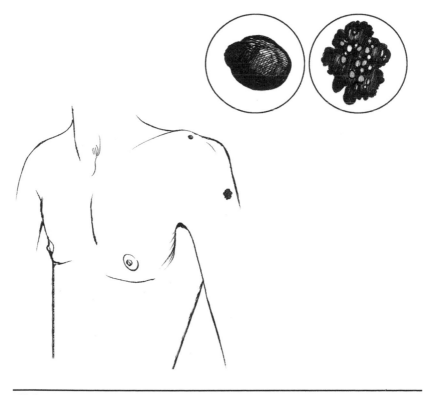

Melanoma

. . . that you've had since you were born

This is known as a congenital nevus (fancy word for mole). These are found in about one out of every 100 people and vary in size. If the mole has a diameter that is eight inches or longer, there is a greater chance of it becoming cancerous. Congenital nevi are more likely to turn into melanoma than moles that appear on the body after birth. These moles can also become hairier and more textured as time progresses— just like every other part of your body. Guess these moles don't age gracefully.

. . . that is the color of coffee with milk

You may have a birthmark known as a café au lait spot. While café au lait birthmarks are generally harmless, if you have six or more that are larger than the size of a quarter, you may have a genetic disorder known as neurofibromatosis, where noncancerous tumors composed of nerve tissues form in the nervous system (such as the brain, the spinal cord, and the nerves). Besides the presence of café au lait birthmarks, other indications of neurofibromatosis include freckles in the groin or armpits, small bumps on the iris, learning disabilities, a short stature, soft bumps that are found on or under the skin, and even a head that is larger than the average head size. There are three types of neurofibromatosis: NF1, which usually appears in childhood, NF2, where benign tumors affect the ears and hearing, and schwannomatosis, which affects people in their twenties and thirties and causes chronic pain in the body. Nothing like café au lait with a splash of neurofibromatosis on the side!

Before you go to the dermatologist and play whack-a-mole on your face . . .

Take a good look at where your mole is located, because it might mean more than you think. According to the Chinese Almanac, which is over 2,000 years old, moles on the face can mean certain things about your personality and your health. A mole on the side of your nose, for example, suggests that you may be more likely to suffer from illnesses, and a mole underneath your lower lip and in the center might mean you suffer from food allergies or eat too much food. Having a mole in the middle of your nose suggests sexual problems, and having a mole in your eyebrow suggests you are intelligent, creative, and artistic. There are twenty-five different positions and meanings that moles can have on the face, and meanings range from having a high IQ, achieving fame at a young age, having weight issues, having arguments with your extended family, and having people in your life who are jealous of your financial wealth. If you combine all twenty-five meanings together, you will have a plot to one Lifetime movie.

. . . that is blue or gray

You may have a birthmark that is known as a Mongolian blue spot. These birthmarks appear at birth or a little bit later, are noncancerous, and are not associated with any illness or disease. Mongolian blue spots are most commonly found on the buttocks, back, shoulders, and base of the spine, and are more often found in darker-skinned people, such as those of East Indian, African, and Asian descent. These birthmarks have irregular shapes, unclear edges, are generally two to eight centimeters wide, and have the same texture as the rest of your skin. No treatment is necessary to treat Mongolian blue spots, and they will usually fade within a few years and disappear by adolescence—just in time for the rest of your skin to go to hell.

These birthmarks have irregular shapes . . .

. . . that is reddish purple

You may have what is known as a port-wine stain. These birthmarks are composed of swollen blood vessels and tend to deepen in color and take on a cobblestone appearance as you age. Port-wine stains are found in around three out of every thousand people and are more common on the face, though they can develop elsewhere on the body. When a port-wine stain is on the lower and upper eyelids, you risk developing glaucoma. In rare occasions, port-wine stains have been signs of Klippel-Trenaunay-Weber syndrome (which also features varicose veins and excessive growth of a limb or bone) and Sturge-Weber syndrome (which also features paralysis on one side, seizures, and learning disabilities). Both Klippel-Trenaunay-Weber syndrome and Sturge-Weber syndrome are present at birth. If you have a port-wine stain on the face, you can try to treat it with laser therapy, or you can pair it with a nice Gorgonzola or Roquefort cheese.

IF YOU HAVE A RASH . . .

. . . that itches

There could be many causes, including psoriasis, chickenpox, hives, eczema, ringworm, pityriasis rosea (an oval lesion that usually begins at the torso and spreads along the skin lines), poison ivy, or scabies (an allergic reaction that appears as thin lines and small bumps or blisters on the skin and is especially itchy at night). Parasitic mites that burrow into the skin and deposit eggs inside of the skin cause the rash. The easiest way to get scabies is from touching a person who also has it, and the most common way scabies is spread is through sexual activity. A person may not notice symptoms of scabies until two months after the infestation, and the resulting itchiness is relentless. Because the infestation begins subtly, the beginning of scabies is often misdiagnosed as pimples, mosquito bites, bedbug bites, or other types of rashes. So if you're looking for a wild night of passion, think twice before you scratch that itch.

. . . made up of three red, itchy spots next to each other

You may have bedbugs. Bedbugs are small, flat, reddish brown, oval-shaped bugs that feed on animal blood and only come out at night. During the day, these bugs will live in the creases of your mattress, headboard, box spring, or any crack and crevice in your home (they can even be found in electrical outlets and light switches). The most common symptom of bedbug bites are not the actual bumps (which simply look like mosquito bites) but that they usually occur in a group of three or four, commonly known as "breakfast, lunch, and dinner." Once you have a bedbug infestation, it can be extremely difficult to prevent further infestation. Bedbugs hide extremely well and can last for months without eating. Your best line of defense is to call an exterminator immediately, before the problem gets out of hand. So instead of just saying "don't let the bedbugs bite," for the love of God, start taking a more proactive step.

. . . that has a rapidly growing and elevated sore in the shape of a ring

You may have a fungal infection known as ringworm. Ringworm is caused by microscopic organisms, known as dermatophytes, that live on the outer layer of dead skin. It comes from direct contact with someone who's infected or something they touched. It's more common in kids than adults. While the center of the sore may appear clear (giving it its ringlike shape), the infection causes scaling, itching, pain, crusting, and areas filled with fluid. The lesions are usually small (ranging from ½" to 1½") and can occur as a single sore or as groups of three or four sores. Ringworm is incredibly contagious, and though it can go away on its own, it can also be cured with antifungal cream. And don't worry—there are no actual worms involved in ringworm. I don't know about you, but I always prefer my medical diagnoses to be like an Ingmar Bergman film: misleading and unclear.

. . . that has a stripe of blisters that wrap around one side of your torso

You may have shingles. The fun thing about shingles is that it's like a visit from an ex. Only this time, they are back with a vengeance. You see, shingles is actually caused by the varicella-zoster virus, which is the same virus that gave you chickenpox as a child (and is also a herpes virus). Once you are through with chickenpox, the virus remains inactive in your nerve tissue near your brain and spinal cord until years later when it re-emerges as the bigger and badder version, shingles. The viral infection gives you an extremely painful and itchy rash on one side of your body, and blisters will form that will break open and crust over. You can have symptoms around the site where the blisters form. Shingles can lead to a loss of vision (if around the eye),

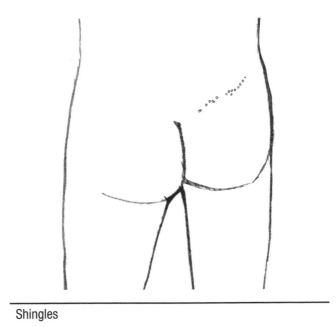

Shingles

facial paralysis, inflammation of the brain, balance and hearing problems, and even postherpetic neuralgia, where the pain continues after the rash has dissipated because your nerve fibers have become damaged and continue to send messages of pain from your skin to your brain. A secondary bacterial infection can even form around the blisters. However, shingles still does not have the ability to emotionally stunt you or take your favorite jacket and never return it. Shingles: 0, Ex: 1.

... that has red sores that ooze and form a yellowish brown crust

You may have a highly contagious bacterial skin infection known as impetigo. Impetigo usually affects children and infants, and it will go away on its own within two or three weeks. The red sores usually appear on the face, especially around the mouth and nose. Impetigo is caused by bacteria (strep or staph) that usually enters the skin via cuts or insect bites. There are three types of impetigo: nonbullous impetigo, bullous impetigo, and ecthyma. Nonbullous impetigo is the most common type of impetigo and features red sores on the face that rupture quickly, ooze pus or fluid, and form a crust that is honey colored. Bullous impetigo usually affects children and infants under the age of two and features fluid-filled, painless blisters. Ecthyma is the most serious type of impetigo. In ecthyma, the infection penetrates the dermis and creates pus and fluid-filled sores that become ulcers. The sores break open, leaving a chance of scarring and intense stares.

> Bullous impetigo usually affects children ...

... after swimming

You probably have swimmer's itch, which is actually grosser than it sounds. You see, when you go swimming in freshwater and sometimes even in saltwater, you can expose your body to small parasites that burrow into your skin. The parasites are normally found in freshwater snails, but they can migrate to ducks, geese, gulls, swans, muskrats, and beavers. The rash usually appears anywhere between two hours and two days after swimming. The good news is that human beings do not make good hosts for these parasites, which begin to die inside of your skin (that's good news, right?). The rash, also known as cercarial dermatitis, is usually gone within a few days, and the itching can be treated with over-the-counter medications. However, while the rash will go away, the thought of dead parasites in your skin may haunt you for several years.

... that is violet

You may have an inflammatory autoimmune disease known as dermatomyositis (meaning skin and muscles). The most distinctive signs of this condition are muscle weakness and a very specific rash. Muscles close to the trunk, such as thighs, hips, shoulders, neck, and upper arms, become progressively weaker over time. The rash, which is violet or dusky red, is commonly found on the face and eyelids, and around the elbows, knuckles, nails, knees, back, and chest. Dermatomyositis is found in women more than men. Adults develop the condition between the ages of forty to sixty, and children develop the condition between the ages of five and fifteen. Other symptoms of dermatomyositis include difficulty swallowing, weight loss, fatigue, fever, lung problems, and hard deposits of calcium that are found under the skin. The muscle weakness associated with dermatomyositis can lead to pneumonia, breathing issues, gastrointestinal problems, a life dedicated to Dungeons and Dragons, and a slim to none chance of encountering the opposite sex.

You may develop a rash on your skin known as pruritic urticarial papules and plaque of pregnancy, or PUPPP. This itchy, bumpy rash develops during your third trimester and is located on your abdomen, particularly around the umbilical area, can move to the thighs and other extremities, and is usually seen in first-time mothers or with those who are carrying more than one child. Its cause is unknown but may be due to extreme stretching of the skin. Having PUPPP does not affect your unborn child in any way, and it will go away after delivering. Though the itching can become very bad, you should not take oral steroids while pregnant. Instead, try relieving symptoms with cold compresses, aloe vera gel, topical creams (though you should seek the attention of a dermatologist to find out the right kind to use), or by taking a bath of baking soda or oatmeal—brown sugar optional.

. . . that appears as red blotches on your wrists, ankles, palms, and the soles of your feet

You may have Rocky Mountain spotted fever. This is a bacterial disease that is actually spread by a tick, and it causes your blood vessels to leak. Rocky Mountain spotted fever can cause serious damage to your internal organs (especially the kidneys), and can even be fatal if not treated early. Symptoms of the disease can take up to fourteen days after exposure to begin showing, and the initial symptoms are very nonspecific (fever, chills, nausea, vomiting, and muscle aches). Following these symptoms, the nonitchy rash develops, usually on the wrists and ankles at first, and then spreads down the arms and legs. Though it was originally identified in the Rocky Mountains, the disease is most common in the southeastern United States, and it is also found in Mexico, South America, Central America, and Canada. Nothing like a disease that's also a world traveler.

Symptoms of the disease can take up to fourteen days after exposure to begin showing . . .

IF YOUR SKIN . . .

. . . has patches that are becoming either lighter or darker in color and are scaling

You may have a fungal infection known as tinea versicolor. The most common areas affected by tinea versicolor are the chest, back, and shoulders, and it mostly affects young adults and adolescents. The infection is caused by *Malassezia furfur*, a yeast found on the skin of most adults that doesn't usually cause any problems; you met this beast earlier in Chapter 2. Tinea versicolor can appear as a few spots on your skin, or there can be so many spots that your skin that isn't affected seems like it is the infected area. The good news is that the infection is easily treatable with over-the-counter medication (including antifungal dandruff shampoos), antifungal cream, or oral treatment. If treated, tinea versicolor will not leave any permanent damage to the skin, which is small consolation to the teen who's just been diagnosed with the infection.

. . . has patches that are milky white

You may have a skin condition known as vitiligo. Vitiligo happens when the cells responsible for producing melanin, the pigment that establishes the color of your eyes, hair, and skin, die off or stop forming melanin. This results in a depigmentation of the skin, which causes these patches of milky-white areas. Vitiligo usually starts to appear between the ages of ten to thirty, and it can occur on any part of the body, though those areas that are exposed to sunlight are more often affected first. There are three patterns vitiligo appears as: focal (where depigmentation only affects one or a few parts of the body), segmental (where depigmentation occurs on only one side of the body), and generalized (where depigmentation is widespread across the body and often symmetrical). Generalized vitiligo is the most common type. Vitiligo is not that *bad* and shouldn't make your life too much of a *thriller*. It can, however, change the *man in the mirror* that you see every day. See what I just did there?

. . . is yellow

You may have jaundice. Jaundice is a yellowing of the skin, eyes, or mucous membranes that occurs from bilirubin, the byproduct created by old red blood cells. Every single day, your body replaces a small amount of old red blood cells with new red blood cells. As the liver gets rid of the old blood cells, bilirubin is formed, and your liver breaks this down so that it can be removed in your stool. If bilirubin begins to build up in the body, this leads to jaundice. Jaundice can be the result of the liver being damaged or overloaded, too many red blood cells dying, or the digestive tract being unable to move the bilirubin in the right way. Often, jaundice is an indication that there might be a problem with your liver, pancreas, or gallbladder— or the lighting in your bathroom.

The ABCs of Hepatitis

Though there are three different types of hepatitis, they all feature jaundice as one of the main symptoms. Hepatitis involves a viral infection that causes an inflamed and swollen liver. Hepatitis A is a liver infection that is highly contagious and usually resolves on its own. A person gets hepatitis A from eating or drinking food that has been contaminated by infected stool. Hepatitis B is spread by being in contact with infected bodily fluids or blood and will also resolve on its own. Hepatitis B is commonly spread by having unprotected sex, getting a tattoo with unclean tools, sharing needles, or sharing toothbrushes or razors. Hepatitis C is the most serious form of hepatitis and can cause permanent damage to the liver, liver cancer, liver failure, and cirrhosis (many don't even know they have the condition until the damage has been done). Hepatitis C is also caused by coming into contact with blood that is infected with the virus, and most of the time it is a long-term condition. There's one alphabet that every hypochondriac will be sure to memorize.

. . . has a protrusion that looks like an animal horn

You could be developing a cutaneous horn. These horns are actually made up of compacted keratin and occur most often at sites where the skin is the most exposed to the sun. The cutaneous horns, which can measure from a few millimeters to up to 5–6 centimeters, start to grow out of a skin lesion, which is usually benign. The elderly and those who are fair-skinned are more likely to develop cutaneous horns. Conditions that may give rise to cutaneous horns are squamous cell carcinoma, basal cell carcinoma, Bowen's disease, Paget's disease, actinic keratosis, and malignant melanoma. For this reason, it is important to have your cutaneous horn checked out to make sure there is not an underlying problem. The most common cause of injury for people with cutaneous horns is the damage done by ramming into other people with a cutaneous horn to show dominance.

. . . is very stretchy and easily damaged

You may have a type of Ehlers-Danlos syndrome. There are actually six major forms of Ehlers-Danlos syndrome, as well as five minor types of the condition. People with Ehlers-Danlos syndrome have genetic mutations that are responsible for disrupting collagen production, a key component for the connective tissue of the body. The most obvious symptoms that a person is suffering from Ehlers-Danlos syndrome include having very fragile and stretchy skin and having extremely flexible joints or being double jointed. Having Ehlers-Danlos syndrome can also lead to damaged blood vessels and, in rare cases, a rupture of the internal organs. While there is no treatment for Ehlers-Danlos syndrome, many who suffer from the condition are able to live a normal, healthy life—as normal as it could be for someone with all that extra skin.

. . . has small, firm, bumpy, red papules on your back or chest

You may have Grover's disease, otherwise known as transient acantholytic dermatosis or persistent acantholytic dermatosis (catchy, no?). The cause of Grover's disease is unknown, though males over the age of fifty are most often affected by it. The papules may itch, blister, and crust over, and there might be some bleeding. It is believed that Grover's disease is caused by sun damage, and it might occur following heat stress or sweating; however, it is also seen in very dry skin. In most cases, Grover's disease only lasts for six to twelve months, but in some cases it may come and go with a seasonal variation. Though there is no cure, itching can be relieved with topical steroids, moisturizing creams, and calcipotriol (synthetic vitamin D) cream. Grover's disease should not be confused with Grover disease, a life-threatening condition where a person develops a round, pink nose and a thick coat of blue fur.

... has red, brown, or purple, round, pinpoint spots

You may have petechiae, which is a sign of bleeding under the skin. The small round dots occur when the capillaries hemorrhage and this blood then leaks into the skin. Petechiae usually appears in clusters and is often found in the feet and ankles where more pressure is applied to the veins. Bleeding in the skin can also appear as larger flat areas (known as purpura) or as one large bruising (known as ecchymosis). Bleeding under the skin can be a sign of many different conditions, and some can be quite serious. Causes of the condition include injury or trauma, leukemia, septicemia (a life-threatening infection caused by bacteria in the blood), and thrombocytopenia (which is a name for disorders that have abnormally low amounts of platelets present). Though petechiae can be frightening, it can actually be fun to connect your own dots and see what appears before your eyes!

This will really make your skin crawl . . .
People suffering from a condition known as Morgellons disease experience extremely bizarre and terrifying symptoms. A person with Morgellons disease will have skin lesions that do not heal, and will have multicolored fibers in and protruding from the skin that create a great itching and burning sensation. But the worst part about Morgellons disease is that people suffering from the disease experience a crawling sensation on their skin that can be compared to bugs moving, biting, and stinging their body. Other symptoms include a swelling of the joints and a loss of hair. Little is known about the disease, and health-care professionals still disagree on whether it is, in fact, a separate disease such as a parasitic infestation, or simply the result of other conditions (more than half of the people diagnosed with Morgellons disease also had Lyme disease). Some even believe it is related to mental illness (there have been cases where people claimed they actually saw bugs flying in and out of their skin, and symptoms of the condition are similar to schizophrenia). Whether Morgellons disease is actually a separate disease or not, a person suffering from the condition definitely has something bugging him or her.

. . . has large, fluid-filled blisters

You may have a rare skin condition known as bullous pemphigoid. These large blisters are the result of your body's immune system attacking a thin layer of tissue that connects the dermis and the epidermis. The blisters contain a clear liquid (though sometimes there is blood inside), do not rupture easily, and are most commonly found on the arms, inner thighs, abdomen, and groin. Other symptoms of bullous pemphigoid include hives and mouth sores. Bullous pemphigoid occurs in people who are age sixty and older, and it is most frequent among people in their eighties. On a positive note, people with bullous pemphigoid can opt out of bringing their AARP cards to the movies, since the proof of their age is already hanging out on their skin.

... has ulcers that have red or purple borders

You may have pyoderma gangrenosum, which starts out as a few small, red bumps that look like spider bites. These then turn into larger open sores, or ulcers, that have borders that are reddish purple in color. The ulcers are typically found on the legs, though they can develop anywhere on the body, and other symptoms include achy joints and bone pain. While little is known about what causes pyoderma gangrenosum, the condition is commonly associated with other inflammatory illnesses such as Crohn's disease, rheumatoid arthritis, hepatitis, and ulcerative colitis. If you have the condition, any time there is a new trauma to the skin such as a wound or a cut, it can result in ulcers. Pyoderma gangrenosum is usually found among people forty to fifty years old. So during your midlife crisis, in between buying the new flashy car and the clothing that doesn't fit properly, make sure you pencil in a doctor's appointment.

The ulcers are typically found on the legs, though they can develop anywhere on the body ...

... has a small, bright red bump

You probably have a cherry hemangioma, otherwise known as Campbell De Morgan spots. These are noncancerous growths that typically develop on people over the age of thirty and usually have a diameter of a quarter inch or less. The more you age, the more cherry hemangiomas you tend to develop. These skin growths are actually the result of an overgrowth of blood vessels, and while they can show up anywhere on the body, they are usually found on the trunk. Though the cause of cherry hemangiomas is unknown, it is believed that genetics plays a role in who does or does not develop them. If you have a cherry hemangioma, there is really no need to worry, unless you hate how it looks. If it really bothers you, go to the doctor and have him pop that cherry.

... itches more when you scratch it

You may have a condition known as neurodermatitis, or scratch dermatitis. One of the most telling signs of scratch dermatitis is when you have a patch of skin that is scaly, leathery, or thick as a result of your chronic scratching. The itchy skin associated with the condition is often found as a single patch on the neck, wrist, forearm, ankle, or thigh, and sometimes the scrotum or vulva can be affected. The direct cause of neurodermatitis remains unknown; however, it has been associated with skin conditions such as psoriasis and eczema. Certain risk factors of neurodermatitis include being a woman, being between the ages of thirty and fifty, and having a family or personal history of skin conditions like psoriasis and eczema. People who have scratch dermatitis may even come to the point where scratching the affected area becomes more of a habit. Sometimes, there really is an itch you can't scratch . . .

Does your skin turn black or green when you wear gold jewelry?

This reaction is known as black dermographism, literally meaning "black writing on the skin," and it is more prevalent in women. For years, many believed this to be a result of an iron deficiency; however, this is not the case. Due to the fact that gold jewelry can't be pure gold because it is too soft, metal alloys such as nickel, silver, zinc, and copper are mixed in and the metal alloy may be reacting to the sulphides and chlorides in your sweat. Some believe black dermographism is a reaction caused by cosmetics in the skin and a metallic abrasion from the metal jewelry. Others, however, believe it is caused by a breakdown of sulfur-containing proteins in the skin and that this is hormonally controlled. I don't know which is right, but I do know that anytime a woman is controlled by hormones, you'd better just get her some gold and get out of the room as fast as possible.

CHAPTER 10

Shoulders

Sure, you might have a good head on your shoulders, but that's where it ends. Illnesses, deformities, and injuries of the shoulder can be incredibly painful and, oftentimes, very noticeable. Whether you have a bump sticking out, a shoulder blade protruding from your back, a hump between your shoulders, or simply a fatty lump in your skin, people are going to take notice. This will make you start looking over your shoulder, thinking everyone is talking about you. Then, you'll start giving people the cold shoulder in retaliation. Soon, you'll have lost all hope for humanity and become a complete misanthrope. And to think, it all could have been fixed by just diagnosing your problem and getting it taken care of. Talk about having a chip on your shoulder . . .

IF THE BACKS OF YOUR SHOULDERS . . .

. . . have a fatty lump between the skin and the muscle

You may have a lipoma. Usually, lipomas are harmless and do not need to be treated unless they are causing you pain or are growing. Lipomas usually have a diameter of two inches, are soft and doughy feeling (they even move if you apply pressure with your finger), and generally occur in the shoulders, neck, back, thighs, and arms. Though the cause of lipomas is unknown, they do tend to run in families, commonly occur between the ages of forty and sixty, and develop in those who already have other disorders like Gardner syndrome, Cowden syndrome, and Madelung's disease. Unfortunately these lumps won't go away unless you have them surgically removed. So if you find yourself stuck with a little doughy piece of fat in your shoulder, just do what you can to make the best of it: Put a chef's hat on it, poke it in the middle a few times, and, voilà, you have your own Pillsbury Doughboy.

. . . have a fatty deposit between them

This is known as a buffalo hump, and it is a symptom of Cushing's syndrome. Cushing's syndrome occurs when the body is exposed to too much or produces too much of the hormone cortisol. The most common cause is from the use of corticosteroid medication (which is prescribed to treat inflammatory diseases like asthma and to prevent rejection of a newly transplanted organ). If caused by the adrenal glands overproducing cortisol, this could mean you have a pituitary gland tumor, an adrenal gland disease, or an ectopic ACTH-secreting tumor (ACTH is the hormone responsible for regulating cortisol). Other symptoms of Cushing's syndrome include weight gain in the upper back, midsection, and face (known as moon face); acne; purple or pink stretch marks on the arms, thighs, breasts, and abdomen; skin that bruises easily; and cuts and infections that heal very slowly. Between buffalo hump and moon face, it's pretty apparent that once Cushing's syndrome came along, doctors stopped giving a crap in the naming department.

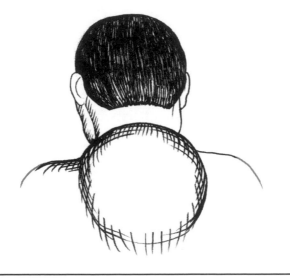

Buffalo hump

. . . protrude from your back

You may have what is known as a winged scapula. Scapula is another term for shoulder blade, and a winged scapula can appear as a result of damaging or having a contusion of the long thoracic nerve or weakening of the serratus anterior muscle. This damage can be the result of a viral infection or a trauma (even one you suffered at birth). The most obvious symptom of a winged scapula is the large protrusion of the shoulder blade in the back, which appears winglike and can be seen when pushing against a wall. Other symptoms include pain or discomfort while elevating the shoulder, and having poor posture due to pressure placed on the scapula while sitting. Rehabilitation of a winged scapula includes exercises to strengthen the serratus anterior muscle; however, in extreme cases, surgery may be required. If you have a winged scapula, this in no way makes you any more birdlike, and it certainly does not mean you have the ability to fly. And if you think you do, perhaps it wasn't just your shoulder that was damaged . . .

Rehabilitation of a winged scapula includes exercises . . .

IF THE SIDE OF YOUR SHOULDER . . .

. . . feels mushy, as if there is no bone present, and is turned upward and backward

You may have dislocated your shoulder out of its socket. When you have a dislocated shoulder, the ball of the joint rips out of the socket, tearing the cartilage, the joint capsule, the rotator cuff, and the ligaments. This makes mobility of your arm extremely difficult—and extremely painful. A partial dislocation is known as a subluxation, and this is when the shoulder marginally slips out of the socket and then immediately goes back to normal. To prevent dislocating your shoulder, avoid hard falls or collisions . . . which hopefully you're doing anyway.

... has a bump at the top

You may have a separated shoulder. When this happens, you have not actually injured your shoulder joint but instead have torn one of the ligaments that connect the shoulder blade to the collarbone. As a result of the tear, the collarbone is no longer anchored and can move out of place. As the collarbone presses against the skin at the top of the shoulder, it creates a deformity. Much like a dislocated shoulder, the most common cause of a separated shoulder is a hard blow or fall on the shoulder. Surgery is not usually required to heal a separated shoulder, and often it will heal on its own within a few weeks if you use a sling. In the meantime, avoid high places and getting into fights.

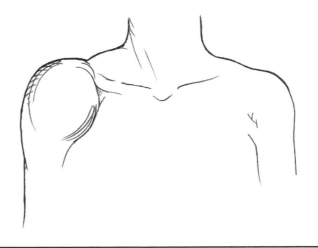

Separated shoulder

... is red or swollen

You may have an inflammation or irritation known as bursitis. Around each joint you have a fluid-filled sac known as the bursa, which decreases friction, irritation, and rubbing. When you get injured or overuse a certain joint, you can irritate and inflame the bursa. Other parts of your body that can be affected by bursitis include your hips, elbows, knees, and Achilles tendons. Pain from bursitis can be extreme, and it can either build up gradually or occur suddenly. Another sign of bursitis is adhesive capsulitis, otherwise known as frozen shoulder, where your shoulder is very stiff and you can't move it. Coincidentally, one of the ways to cure a frozen shoulder is to ice it. Pretty ironic, right?

Freeze Frame

A frozen shoulder can last for up to two years, and treatment usually involves physical therapy and sometimes the use of numbing medications or corticosteroids. However, another alternative form of treatment is called transcutaneous electrical nerve stimulation (or TENS). This involves delivering small electrical currents to the key areas on the pathway of the nerves. Though the reason for why this helps a frozen shoulder is still unknown, it is believed that endorphins might be released upon being stimulated, that pain fibers (which carry the impulses of pain) are blocked, or because this technique may simulate acupuncture meridians. Even though the electrical currents don't actually hurt or cause any pain, that doesn't give your doctor the right to say "I'm sorry, the governor didn't call" right before you start . . .

CHAPTER 11

Back

Back for more, huh? Back problems can cause a lifetime of pain and discomfort if not identified and treated properly. In other words, the symptoms you'll find in this chapter are not ones that you should turn your back on, because if you do, you might end up with your back against the wall later on in life. Conditions and illnesses that affect your back can lead to a permanent curvature of one side, a hunched over position, and even an inability to lift your head! If you start to show symptoms, your best bet is to figure out what's wrong and get seen by a doctor. They've always got your back.

IF YOUR LOWER BACK . . .

. . . has a craterlike ulcer

Houston, we have a problem, because you may have a bedsore. Bedsores, also known as pressure ulcers, occur when blood supply to the skin has been cut off for a prolonged amount of time, leading to death of the skin and tissue. There are four stages of bedsores: (1) pink or dark discoloration that is possibly tender and itchy, (2) swollen, red skin with open areas or blisters, (3) a craterlike ulcer that goes deep into the skin and has yellow, dead skin, and (4) a craterlike ulcer that goes even deeper into the skin, going to the muscle, deep fat, and even bone. In stage four, you will also have an eschar, which is crusty, black, dead tissue. So unless you want your doctors to re-enact the moon landing on your back, get up and walk around every once in a while.

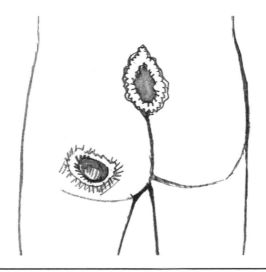

Bedsore

... hurts and you have a red circle that looks like a bull's-eye on your body

Take a good look at that circle, because there might be a bug bite in there. To be a little more precise, the bug in question is a spirochaete, a bacteria which has infected a deer tick (which does the biting), and the illness you now may have is Lyme disease. These red circles (called erythema migrans) can appear in places beyond where the tick has bitten you as the spirochaete travels through the skin and will usually appear one to four weeks from the time you were bitten. Other symptoms of Lyme disease include flulike symptoms, joint pain and swelling (especially in the knees), and sometimes, Bell's palsy (when one side of your face becomes temporarily paralyzed), meningitis (a swelling of the membranes that surround the brain), and even an irregular heartbeat. Deer ticks may be small (the size of a sesame seed), but they pack a powerful punch. So the next time you decide to go frolic in the woods, remember to use bug spray, tuck your pants into your socks, have a set of tweezers on hand, and let your paranoia run wild. Nothing like getting out there and experiencing nature.

> Deer ticks may be small, but they pack a powerful punch.

. . . curves too far inward

You may have lordosis, also known as swayback, which can cause pain and can even affect a person's ability to move. Lordosis can be caused by certain conditions such as obesity, achondroplasia (a disorder that affects bone growth and is the most common type of dwarfism), osteoporosis, discitis (an inflammation of the disc space or intervertebral disc), and spondylolisthesis (where vertebra in the lower back shift out of place). If the curve caused by lordosis reverses when you bend over, there is no need to be concerned. If, however, the lordosis remains when you bend over, this means the lordosis may need to be treated. One common symptom of the inward curve is a more prominent-looking buttocks. So you may have a swayback, but at least you're filling out those jeans.

... has a lump

You may have kidney cancer, also known as renal cancer, where the kidney cells start to become malignant and a tumor begins to form. The cancerous lump on the kidney can also protrude into the abdomen. The most common form of kidney cancer in adults is renal cell carcinoma, which is when the cancer initially forms at the lining of the tubules, the tiny tubes within the kidney. There are rarely any early signs of renal cell carcinoma; however, other symptoms of the condition include blood in the urine, anemia, a swelling of the legs or ankles, a pain that is located on your side that never seems to go away, weight loss, and having a fever for weeks without having a cold or infection. Certain risk factors for kidney cancer include being male, being black, being obese, being older than forty, smoking, using medications for a long period of time, having lymphoma, and having a kidney.

IF YOUR UPPER BACK . . .

... has flat brown, black, or gray spots

You may have age spots, also known as liver spots. Age spots occur in areas of the body that receive the most exposure to the sun and are commonly found on the upper back, shoulders, face, arms, and hands. Age spots are more commonly found in people over the age of forty and vary in size. It should be noted that while age spots are usually noncancerous, they should be medically evaluated because any change in appearance, shade, or size can be a sign of a melanoma (see Chapter 9). The best way to avoid having age spots is to protect your skin from the sun. Age spots are more of a cosmetic issue than anything else and are really just a nuisance. Kind of like when your mother always told you to wear sunscreen when you went to the beach . . . oh wait . . .

. . . has a hump

You may have kyphosis, also known as hunchback or round back. Though rounding of the back is natural, people with kyphosis have a rounding of over 50 degrees. Kyphosis can be the result of many things, including trauma, degenerative diseases like arthritis of the spine, osteoporosis (a bone-thinning disease), tumors, and spina bifida (a birth defect where part of the spine has not completely fused, leaving it split). In severe cases of kyphosis, your organs, tissues, nerves, and lungs can all be affected due to compression. Kyphosis can affect people of all ages, and the most common type is known as postural kyphosis, which usually appears during adolescence. Now if only there was a famous hunchback we could discuss here . . . maybe someone French . . .

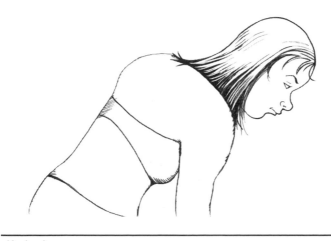

Kyphosis

IF YOUR WHOLE BACK . . .

. . . makes it impossible for you to lift your head up

You may have an inflammatory disease known as ankylosing spondylitis. Ankylosing spondylitis causes vertebrae in your spine to actually fuse together. This makes the spine much less flexible and can leave a person in a hunched-forward position. In severe cases of ankylosing spondylitis, a person might not be able to lift his or her head enough even to look forward. Men are affected with ankylosing spondylitis much more than women, and symptoms usually start to show in early adulthood. Early symptoms of the condition include stiffness and pain in the hips and lower back, as well as inflammation. The fusion of the bone occurs when new bone starts to form in an attempt to heal itself from the inflammation this disease causes. The newly formed bone begins to bridge the gap between the vertebrae, and as a result, it fuses parts together. But look on the bright side; think of all the change you'll find as you're looking down at the sidewalk!

> Early symptoms . . . include stiffness and pain in the hips . . .

. . . has V-shaped stripes

You may have what are known as Blaschko's lines. Don't be alarmed yet; these lines are actually found on everyone, but most of the time they are *invisible* (NOW you should be alarmed). It is believed that Blaschko's lines trace the migration path of embryonic cells, are built into our DNA, and are not related to the lymphatic, muscular, or nervous systems. Even more interestingly, these lines can clearly be seen in dogs, cats, and other animals. The only reason your back looks like a tiger right now is because you have some underlying condition that is presenting itself through these lines. Conditions that can make Blaschko's lines present include lichen planus, lichen striatus, and lupus erythematosus. When seen on the back, these stripes appear as a V-shape, and when found on the stomach, chest, or sides, these stripes are S-shaped. Though these stripes may make you look like more of an animal, that still doesn't give you an excuse to start peeing in public . . .

. . . curves to one side

You may have scoliosis. The cause of scoliosis remains mostly unknown; however, it occurs most frequently right before puberty when there is a growth spurt and in people who suffer from conditions like muscular dystrophy and cerebral palsy. While most cases of scoliosis are mild, if you have a severe case, scoliosis can be debilitating and can even affect the way your lungs function and your ability to breathe. The most obvious way to see if you or someone else has scoliosis is to look at these signs: one shoulder and/or hip higher than the others, and/or a shoulder blade that seems more prominent than the other shoulder. If the scoliosis progresses, the spine will not only curve to one side, but it will also twist, making the ribs on one side protrude more than the ribs on the other side. Just when puberty couldn't get any meaner, it throws a curveball at you. Well, more specifically, at your spine.

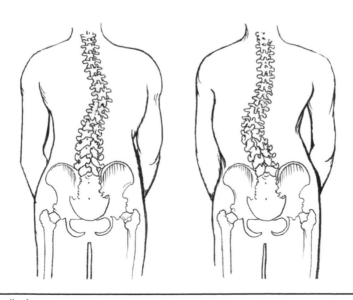

Scoliosis

How's your posture?

You may slouch because it feels more comfortable, but in the long run, it can really end up hurting you. Drooping your head and shoulders forward increases pressure, creating stress on the muscles of your head, neck, and spine. Bad posture can lead to headaches; back, neck, and shoulder pain; difficulty breathing; high blood pressure; bone spurs (protrusions along the edges of bones that cause pain when rubbed against tendons, bones, and nerves); and damage to intervertebral discs (these discs lie between the vertebrae and will bulge or protrude, causing back pain as the gel-like cushion of the discs presses against nerves of the spine or the spinal cord). Intervertebral disc damage can even lead to the inability to move. Sitting and standing straighter also demonstrates a sense of confidence, which you certainly won't have if you spend all day worrying why your body is all out of whack.

CHAPTER 12

Arms

Occasionally, finding symptoms can leave you up in arms . . . After all, who wouldn't be upset if they saw bumps, lumps, scales, swelling, and lesions coming out of two of their major extremities? The Second Amendment of the United States Constitution clearly states it is your right to keep and bear arms, so you do whatever you can to make sure that happens. If you think you have Churg-Strauss syndrome, ichthyosis vulgaris, or anything else that endangers that constitutional right, you definitely want to make sure you go to your doctor and have that checked out. So take a look through this chapter and start self-diagnosing!

IF YOUR UPPER ARM . . .

. . . has a bulbous swelling when you flex

This is a sign of a distal biceps tendon rupture. The biceps muscle goes from the shoulder to the elbow—on the inside of the arm—and it primarily helps bend the elbow. When your biceps tendon ruptures, you'll be sure to know it, and you'll most certainly know the reason why it happened (something hit you, and it hit you hard). A distal biceps tendon rupture can also occur when gravity works against you as your arm is bent (for example, trying to catch a heavy object as it falls). One of the most obvious symptoms of a distal biceps tendon rupture is the loud snap you will hear coming from the elbow, followed by pain and bruising. Maybe the snap you'll hear is your body's way of naturally setting a tempo to the screaming that follows.

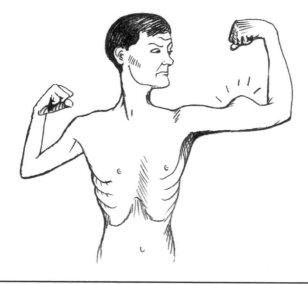

Distal biceps tendon rupture

. . . is swollen

You may have a condition known as lymphedema. Lymphedema, which refers to the swelling of usually one arm or leg, is the result of a blockage in the lymphatic system that inhibits lymph fluid from draining properly and results in a buildup of the lymph fluid. The most common cause of lymphedema is damage or removal of the lymph nodes due to cancer treatment (especially breast cancer). Lymphedema can be caused on its own (known as primary lymphedema) or as a result of another condition or illness (known as secondary lymphedema). Causes of primary lymphedema include Milroy's disease (where the lymph nodes form abnormally), Meige's disease (where the lymph vessels form without valves, making drainage difficult), and late onset lymphedema tarda. Causes of secondary lymphedema include cancer, surgery, infection, radiation treatment, and getting punched in the arm over and over again.

> Causes of secondary lymphedema include cancer . . .

. . . has coin-shaped, raised lesions

You may have a type of eczema known as nummular dermatitis. While the cause of these lesions is unknown, it is believed that the same things that trigger other kinds of eczema can trigger nummular dermatitis. These include frequently bathing, using soaps that irritate or dry out your skin, and exposing yourself to certain types of fabric, like wool. The coin-shaped lesions caused by nummular dermatitis are itchy, scaly, and often feature small breaks in the skin. The lesions are usually found on the arms and legs, and are the most severe during the wintertime, which is when these lesions usually appear. Men usually have the condition more than women, and, for men, the first outbreak of nummular dermatitis typically occurs between the ages of fifty-five and sixty-five. If a woman has the condition, symptoms will usually appear as a teenager. Sometimes nummular dermatitis is a chronic condition, meaning the symptoms can recur. It's true, nummular dermatitis can come back just like a bad penny—which is more than appropriate considering that that's just what it looks like.

This is actually one of the earliest symptoms of Parkinson's disease. Other early symptoms of the disease include tremors, rigidity, and bradykinesia, a slowness in initiating and continuing movements. Rigidity occurs when there is more resistance and stiffness as someone else tries to move your joint (a common diagnostic tool for Parkinson's), while bradykinesia occurs when movement is slowed down when performing a certain task or there is a decrease in the motion of an unplanned movement (such as swinging your arms when walking). Other examples of bradykinesia include a decrease in blink rate, having less facial expressions, having a softer speech, and something known as micrographia, which is actually when your handwriting gets smaller. Scientists have found that signals transmitted from dopamine, a hormone and neurotransmitter found in foods like bananas, almonds, and chocolate, are responsible for the normal smooth movement, and that with Parkinson's disease, the nerve cells that release dopamine are destroyed. Just what we need, right? Another excuse to eat chocolate.

IF YOUR LOWER ARM . . .

...becomes very swollen and then thickens and hardens

You may have a rare tropical disease known as lymphatic filariasis. This disease is caused by microscopic, parasitic, threadlike worms that invade the lymph system (which is responsible for fighting infections and maintaining the body's fluid balance) and is spread by infected mosquitoes. As the parasitic larvae enter your system, it can take six to twelve months for them to become fully grown, and then they live inside the human host for several years, producing millions of microfilariae. When that person is bitten by another mosquito, the mosquito ingests these microfilariae and carries them to the next human host. Symptoms of this disease include tissue damage, infections, swelling, and scarring. Those who suffer with lymphatic filariasis are at risk of getting elephantiasis, which creates an incredibly large amount of swelling that can lead to immobility and disfigurement, as well as testicular hydrocele, where the scrotum becomes severely enlarged . . . but don't get your hopes up, guys; it also becomes disfigured. Looks like it's back to the spam e-mails for you.

. . . has a painless red lump

You may have a skin infection known as sporotrichosis. Sporotrichosis occurs most frequently in gardeners, farmers, and horticulturists, because the cause of the infection is a fungus commonly found in vegetation (in particular, the fungus can be found in rose thorns, soil, hay, and even on twigs). If the skin is broken (which can occur as a result of handling the plant materials), the fungus can enter and infect the skin. A small, red lump will develop after the infection (though it can take up to three months before the lump shows itself). While this is usually painless, the lump can turn into an ulcer. The infection can travel up and down the arm, and the resulting sores will not go away unless they are properly treated, and even then, you can have them for years. And you thought gardening was a relaxing hobby . . .

. . . is twitching

Don't panic. This is most likely just a normal reaction. The most common causes of muscle twitching (also known as fasciculations) include dehydration, vitamin deficiency, magnesium deficiency, and exercise. Muscle twitches can also be caused by certain types of medication and drugs like caffeine, Ritalin, amphetamines, Sudafed, and albuterol (an asthma bronchodilator). Muscle twitches can also be linked to certain diseases and life-threatening issues, and may be a symptom of things like rabies, Parkinson's disease, poisoning, muscular dystrophy, and amyotrophic lateral sclerosis (also known as ALS, or Lou Gehrig's disease). Lastly, muscle twitching can occur when you are under great amounts of stress or anxiety. Between trying to figure out if you have Parkinson's, muscular dystrophy, or ALS, how could you not be stressed?

. . . is shaking

You may be experiencing a tremor. Tremors, though more common in older people, can be experienced by anyone. They can be caused by a number of nonmedical things such as aging, weakness of the muscle, low blood sugar, too much caffeine, too much alcohol, not enough magnesium, alcohol withdrawal, anxiety, fatigue, and stress. Tremors can also be caused by a brain tumor, a stroke, Parkinson's disease, an overactive thyroid, multiple sclerosis, nerve impairment, movement problems, and brain disorders. Tremors can be classified as resting (where the tremor is present when your muscles are at rest and goes away when you move your muscles), intentional (where the tremors occur at the end of movement and disappear when at rest), postural (when you have tremors after holding your arm or leg in a certain position for an extended period of time), and essential (the most common type that everyone has, though sometimes it is so small that you don't notice it). The fifth and final type of tremor is known as an underground tremor, and symptoms of this condition include living underground, looking like a giant eel, consumption of living people, and a strong presence of Kevin Bacon. Wait, that's a movie? Oh . . .

. . . has a bone puncturing through the skin

It's pretty safe to say you have broken your arm. Of course, there are other symptoms of a broken arm, such as swelling, your arm now being deformed when compared to your other arm, an inability to move your arm, and, of course, the inevitable pain. A broken arm is also a great way to gauge your level of popularity or learn how self-centered everyone else in the room is. With the power of your cast, the masses will be at your feet, begging to sign their name or write expressions of sorrow onto your arm. Long lines of people will go around the corner of the building as they anxiously await their turn to put their name on you! Oh, the power! Note: a Velcro brace doesn't hold the same appeal for the masses, so make sure you cast up.

Some Alarming Terminology!

It should be noted that a broken arm is a very vague term and can be "broken" down into many possible diagnoses. For example, breaking your bone and not having an open wound is known as a closed fracture, while breaking your bone and having an open wound (or having the bone stick out) is known as an open fracture. If you break your bone and the pieces do not align, this is known as a displaced fracture. When your bone is broken into many pieces, this is a comminuted fracture. A greenstick fracture, which is found in children, is when the fracture does not go all the way through the bone and only one side is broken. A pathologic fracture is when a bone is broken due to the bone being weak. An impacted fracture is when the ends of your bones are wedged into each other. Whew! Try keeping all that straight!

IF YOUR ELBOW . . .

. . . has a raised and solid bump found on or in the skin and is wider than 10 millimeters

This is known as a nodule and can be a symptom of Churg-Strauss syndrome, a disorder featuring an inflammation of the blood vessels (vasculitis). This inflammation can actually cause permanent damage to the tissues and vital organs by restricting blood flow. There are three phases of the condition: the allergic phase (where, first and foremost, you will develop asthma and may suffer from hay fever, sinusitis, and nasal polyps), the eosinophilic phase (where an abnormally large amount of white blood cells are found in the blood or tissue, creating damage), and the vasculitic phase (which features blood vessel inflammation, leading to damage of tissues and vital organs, as well as rashes, swelling, blood in the urine, and nodules at sites of pressure, such as your elbow). At one point in time, there was a fourth and final phase, but doctors decided "panic phase" sounded too frightening.

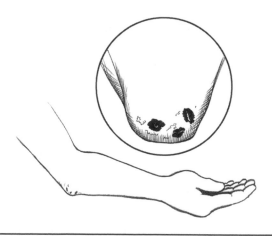

Churg-Strauss syndrome

... has scales

You may have ichthyosis vulgaris, otherwise known as the fish scale disease. This is an inherited disorder where dead skin cells begin to accumulate in thick scales on the body. While some people are born with signs of ichthyosis vulgaris, others may develop symptoms during childhood, and sometimes these symptoms will disappear for much of adulthood and then return. Scales from ichthyosis vulgaris usually appear on the elbows and lower legs. A rare type of ichthyosis that is not caused by genetic abnormalities is known as acquired ichthyosis, and it usually begins in adulthood and is associated with cancer, chronic renal failure, or thyroid disease. There is currently no cure for fish scale disease, though with the aid of several medications (not including fish oil), people suffering from the condition are able to live a normal, happy life within the confines of their aquarium.

... is inflamed and you have a weak grip

You need to put down your racket and take a breather, because you may have lateral epicondylitis, otherwise known as tennis elbow. This condition is painful and occurs from overworking your tendons with a repetitive motion. It is known as tennis elbow because having poor technique in performing a backhand stroke will most certainly lead to this condition. It should be noted, however, that athletes and non-athletes alike can get tennis elbow, and mundane activities like using plumbing equipment, cutting meat, painting, and even using

> This condition is painful and occurs from overworking your tendons with a repetitive motion.

the computer mouse too much can all lead to the inflammation. Tennis elbow is most common in people thirty to fifty years old and in people whose jobs require repetitive motions of the arms and wrists like computer programmers, plumbers, butchers, and adult film stars.

Not ready to put down the tennis racket quite yet? Try acupuncture!

Yes, acupuncture. Now, before you immediately close this book at the thought of small needles being shoved into your body, let's just take a moment to see what it's all about. Acupuncture has been around for thousands of years. Invented in China, those who believed in Traditional Chinese theory inserted needles into certain areas of the body as a method to balance the flow of energy, also known as qi or chi, in the body. It is believed that these parts of the body, known as meridians, are actually parts that stimulate nerves, connective tissue, and muscle, and by placing needles into these areas, it increases blood flow and stimulates the natural painkillers the body has. Acupuncture has been proven to alleviate symptoms of tennis elbow, osteoarthritis, lower back pain, fibromyalgia, migraines, menstrual cramps, and even nausea and vomiting induced by chemotherapy. And if it doesn't work, I imagine you'll be too focused on the *"Oh my god! There are needles in my arm!"* factor to even *notice* what's going on with your elbow. Money well spent.

. . . has red bumps that are raised and resemble a ring

You may have granuloma annulare, a chronic skin condition that commonly affects the elbows, knees, hands, and feet. The pattern of the lesions associated with granuloma annulare may resemble ringworm and may cause pain and itching (though usually these side effects are rare). While unsightly, granuloma annulare causes no real threat to your health and usually goes away within two years. Many people who get granuloma annulare do not have any underlying illnesses; however, the condition has been associated with diabetes mellitus and thyroid disease. Women are twice as likely to get the condition, and if you are over the age of forty, you are at a greater risk of having granuloma annulare that is widespread throughout the body. So, ladies, the next time you say you want a ring on that hand . . . you should be a bit more specific.

IF YOUR WRIST . . .

. . . is deformed

You may have Madelung's deformity, which can lead to pain and limited motion of the wrist. The cause of Madelung's deformity is unknown, but the condition is found in girls more often than boys, and in general, both wrists are affected. Typically, the changes in the wrist do not occur until someone is in his or her early teens. Madelung's deformity can be a symptom of an underlying illness, such as Bessel-Hagen disease (which involves multiple tumors comprised of cartilage), nail-patella syndrome (which involves a series of abnormalities, including an absent kneecap; see the entry in Chapter 20), Leri-Weill syndrome (a genetic disorder characterized by short forearms), and Langer mesomelic dysplasia (a genetic disorder that features dwarfism). Madelung's deformity can be treated surgically, or you can always just pile on the bracelets—or armbands if you'd prefer—to draw attention away from your wrist.

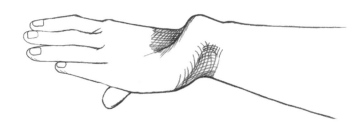

Madelung's deformity

... is swollen, red, and stiff

You may have arthritis. There are more than 100 types of arthritis, which is an inflammation of the area where two bones meet (this is known as a joint). In the most common form of arthritis, known as osteoarthritis, the cartilage that protects the joints wears away, allowing the bones to rub together, which creates inflammation, pain, and stiffness. Nearly 21 million Americans suffer from osteoarthritis, and most people sixty years old or older have some form of the condition. Risk factors such as obesity, overuse of a joint (especially in former athletes), injury, and heredity can lead to osteoporosis. While arthritis cannot be treated, you can reduce discomfort with preventative measures such as certain types of exercise, loss of weight, meditation, and use of over-the-counter medication to relieve pain. Arthritis is kind of like your body's way of telling you, "Hey, I'm too old for this."

. . . has a swollen tendon that is noticeable when making a fist

You may have tendonitis of the thumb, also known as De Quervain's tendonitis. This occurs when the tendons found at the base of your thumb become inflamed or irritated. This can become very painful when using your wrist or thumb (especially when making a fist or holding objects) because the tunnel that surrounds your tendons also starts to swell. Generally, the irritation at the base of your thumb occurs from doing a new motion or activity repeatedly (for example, new mothers, not being used to the particular ways they have to hold a child when caring for them, often get De Quervain's tendonitis). De Quervain's tendonitis can also be triggered by a strain or fracture, which changes the way you normally move your wrist, placing more stress on your tendons. What can we take away from De Quervain's tendonitis? Mother Nature doesn't want you making fists. Make love, not war. On the other hand, making love can lead to having a baby, which can also lead to De Quervain's tendonitis . . . Well played, Mother Nature. Well played.

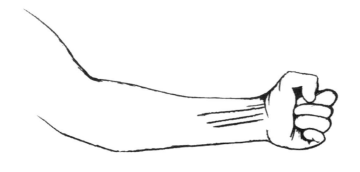

Thumb tendonitis

... has involuntary spasms

You've likely got something called the yips. The yips are most commonly seen in golfers when trying to putt, and it was long believed that they were related to performance anxiety. Recent studies, however, have shown that the yips are actually a result of a neurological dysfunction known as focal dystonia, which can be the result of a magnesium deficiency. This condition is responsible for involuntary muscle spasms that occur when trying to perform a certain task, and the overuse of certain muscles is most likely related to focal dystonia. Anxiety has been shown to worsen the condition, and the combination of anxiety, stress, high-pressure environments, and focal dystonia can turn your birdie into a bogey.

> The irritation at the base of your thumb occurs from doing a new motion or activity repeatedly.

... has a bony lump

This could be a sign of carpal bossing. Though it may be frightening to discover a hard lump on your wrist, a carpal boss is not cancerous. Instead, it is a bone growth that is usually seen after someone hits or injures the back of his or her wrist. Unlike ganglion cysts, which are similar in appearance, a carpal boss is much firmer and cannot be moved. Carpal bosses are similar to bone spurs, and while they are not usually bothersome, the extra bone can be removed surgically, though there is the possibility that it will grow back. Just think of carpal boss as one more unpleasant boss that you have to deal with on a daily basis.

Swans and Frogs and Snakes . . . Oh My!

In ayurvedic medicine, special attention is paid to the wrist—specifically, the pulse. From touching the pulse of both wrists with the index, middle, and ring fingers, ayurvedic practitioners believe they can determine the health of your organs and any potential health problems you may have or will encounter down the line. If the pulse is stronger under the index finger, your pulse will be irregular and moving in waves. This is known as the snake pulse, and it is a sign that your Vata, an energy believed to control body movement, is strong. When the pulse under the middle finger is strongest, it will be active and jumping, and for this reason, it is known as a frog pulse, and it means your Pitta (the energy responsible for your metabolism) is dominant. If the pulse under the ring finger is most noticeable, this will be strong and resemble a floating sensation. This is known as the swan pulse and is a sign that your Kapha (the energy that is responsible for the structure of the body) is dominant. Who knew that you practically had a zoo on your wrist? You better make sure your watch isn't on too tight; you don't want to suffocate a frog . . .

... has itchy, flat-topped, purplish bumps

You may have a common skin disease known as lichen planus. The flat-topped, purplish bumps associated with the condition usually develop on the inner wrist, inner ankles, back, and forearms. The condition can develop on the inside of the mouth as sores or white dots and white lines, and even the fingernails and toenails can be affected (look for ridging and splitting of the nails; in severe cases, lichen planus can actually destroy the entire nail). As the skin disease advances, the purplish bumps on the skin dry out, become scaly, and can develop white lines that go through them (this is known as Wickham's striae). While the cause of the condition is unknown, studies have found an association between lichen planus and hepatitis C. Lichen planus occurs most often in people from thirty to sixty years old, which is nice because nothing cures those thirtieth birthday blues quite like developing a noticeable skin condition . . .

CHAPTER 13

Hands

Now it's time to take a more hands-on approach to the self-diagnosing process. And by hands-on, I mean asking yourself, "What the hell is on my hands?" You see, your hands can tell you all sorts of fun facts about your body, like whether or not you are receiving enough oxygen, or whether you suffer from disorders like hypothyroidism, acromegaly, or Proteus syndrome. Before your symptoms get any worse, take a look and try to discover the root of the problem. That way, you'll be able to get the proper treatment before things gets too out of hand.

IF YOUR HANDS . . .

. . . are swollen

This can be due to a number of reasons. Hand swelling means there is either an inflammation of the joints or tissues in your hand, or there is a buildup of fluid. The swelling could be a result of a trauma, an infection, carpal tunnel syndrome, or serious disorders like arthritis, bursitis, cellulitis, hypothyroidism, hyponatremia (where you have very low sodium), or Kawasaki disease (which involves an inflammation of blood vessels). Your hands can also become swollen from use of certain medications like antidepressants, steroids, hormones, and medication used for high blood pressure and diabetes. Complications can arise from a swelling of the hand, and it can even lead to amputation, weakness, and deformity. Hand swelling can also be due to fluid retention from being pregnant. So hold the applause and get yourself to a doctor!

. . . slowly become more deformed

You most likely have Dupuytren's contracture, where knots of tissue form under the skin of your palm and eventually join together to create a thick cord that will pull one or many fingers and place them in a bent position. Even though "cords" are created, this is not a disease of the tendons of the fingers. Once this occurs, your fingers cannot be straightened. This disorder develops over decades, and early signs include a thickening of the skin in your palm and a firm, sensitive lump of tissue on the palm. Commonly, it is the ring finger and pinky that are affected, and if it appears in both hands, usually one hand is more severe. Smoking and diabetes increase the risk of having Dupuytren's contracture, and men and those of northern European descent are more likely to get this disorder. And if you're a man who is of northern European descent, just accept the inevitability because you're screwed.

> This disorder develops over decades, and early signs include a thickening of the skin in your palm and a firm, sensitive lump of tissue on the palm.

... have solid lumps

This could be a number of different things, and usually these are harmless. Most of the time, these solid lumps are just a malfunction in the amount of cells that have been created for that part of the hand. Different types of lumps include a giant cell tumor (the most common lump found in hands, which, despite its frightening name, is benign and simply made up of the cells from the joint capsule or the lining of the tendon sheath), lipoma (which is comprised of fat cells and usually not common in the hand), fibroma (which is comprised of fibrous cells and is associated with injury), and neuroma (which is comprised of nerve cells and can be painless or lead to some pain and numbing). People with solid lumps in their hand also have a significant disadvantage when it comes to making shadow puppets.

... have a painless lump

You may have a noncancerous cyst known as a ganglion. These usually do not hurt or need treatment, and they grow along the joints or tendons of your hand or wrist. Ganglions occur more often in women, and having injured your tendons or joints or having osteoarthritis puts you at greater risk for getting them. There are four types of ganglion: volar wrist ganglion (cysts that form on the front of the wrist), dorsal wrist ganglion (cysts that form on the back of the wrist), mucous cyst (cysts that form on the last digit of your finger, behind your nail), and pulley, or seed, ganglion (cysts that form in the palm at the base of the fingers). Wrist and seed ganglia will usually go away on their own in a gradual process or burst, dorsal wrist ganglia can take up to five years to go away, and usually surgery is needed to get rid of mucous cysts. If you develop a ganglion, make the best out of the situation. Draw a smiley face on it, start talking to it, and watch as all of the seats in the bus, subway, and restaurant magically clear out.

. . . are blue

This is most likely due to a lack of oxygen in your bloodstream or is the result of very cold temperatures. Cyanosis is the technical term for when the skin turns blue, and this can occur when at a very high altitude, when choking, or it may be a sign of an underlying condition like heart diseases or lung diseases (like asthma, bronchiolitis, croup, pulmonary hypertension, pneumonia, Raynaud's phenomenon, Raynaud's disease, and chronic obstructive pulmonary disease). Blue hands can be a sign of life-threatening conditions like cardiopulmonary arrest (where the heart and lungs have stopped), a pulmonary embolism (a blockage in one of the lung's arteries), cardiovascular disease (heart disease), and epiglottitis (where the epiglottis swells up). Even though having blue hands can be serious, you should take some time out of your day and take some photos (preferably in the car . . . on the way to the hospital). It's like you have real Smurfs! And they're attached to you!

. . . are enlarged

You may have a rare hormonal disorder known as acromegaly. Acromegaly develops when the pituitary gland produces too much growth hormone, which is almost always the result of a benign tumor. The growth hormone plays a key role in regeneration and growth of bone and tissue, but when you have acromegaly the growth hormone causes thickening of the skin, tissue growth, swelling, and bone enlargement. Symptoms of acromegaly include large facial features, enlarged feet and hands, a husky or deep-sounding voice, barrel chest, an enlarged tongue, sleep apnea, thickened and oily skin, and a protrusion of the lower jaw that creates an underbite. People commonly begin experiencing symptoms of acromegaly in middle age. While treatment cannot reverse the excess bone enlargement, it can prevent further growth from happening. If left untreated, however, acromegaly can lead to high blood pressure, heart disease, diabetes, spinal cord compression, and the ability to smell the blood of an Englishman.

The Elephant in the Room

People suffering from the extremely rare congenital disorder known as Proteus syndrome experience an overgrowth of muscle tissues, fatty tissues, blood, bone, skin, and organs. The most famous person to have suffered from Proteus syndrome was Joseph Merrick, otherwise known as the "Elephant man." Though Proteus syndrome is a congenital disorder, it is a progressive illness, meaning that symptoms develop over time and are not immediately present at birth. Other symptoms of Proteus syndrome include having an extremely large head, hands, and feet; having the overgrowth only occur on one side of the body; having raised and rough skin; the development of tumors (including lipomas, tumors made of fatty tissue); having deep-vein thrombosis; and the presence of deep lines on the bottom of the feet. Proteus syndrome is named after the Greek god, Proteus, who had the ability to change his shape whenever he wanted, and in terms of naming a disease, this one couldn't be farther from the truth.

...are red and inflamed

You may have a form of arthritis known as gout, which leads to severe pain, tenderness, and redness of the joints. Gout occurs when uric acid, a chemical produced in the blood and tissue, begins to form needlelike urate crystals around the joints. The most common sites of gout include the joints of the hands, wrist, feet (especially the joint of the big toe), elbows, ankles, and knees. Often, the pain associated with gout develops overnight. For some people, they may only experience gout one time, but people who suffer from recurrent gout can have it several times a year. If gout goes untreated, the urate crystals can form underneath the skin (these are called tophi)—just like one of those grow-your-own crystals sets you had as a kid.

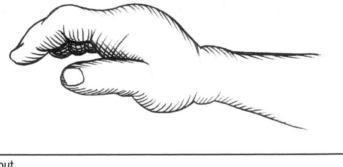

Gout

...have small fluid-filled blisters

You may have dyshidrotic eczema, or dyshidrosis, a skin condition that affects the palms of the hand, fingers, and soles of the feet. The blisters create an intense itching and the rash associated with dyshidrosis can last for about three weeks. The cause of dyshidrosis is unknown, but it is sometimes associated with atopic dermatitis and allergy-related conditions such as hay fever. In dyshidrosis, the skin becomes inflamed, and the spaces between the skin cells open. In a process known as spongiosis, these spaces are then filled with a fluid known as serum. When these blisters begin to dry, painful fissures (or cracks and grooves) start to form. Women, people who are under stress, people who have seasonal allergies, and anyone who is frequently exposed to moisture and metal salts are at a greater risk of having the skin condition. The good news is that you can finally say that you've had something "in the palm of your hand." The bad news: all you have are blisters.

> When these blisters begin to dry, painful fissures (or cracks and grooves) start to form.

...are moving involuntarily

You may have a rare neurological condition known as alien hand syndrome or Dr. Strangelove syndrome. While people with alien hand syndrome experience sensation in the affected hand, they are not able to control the movements of the hand, and they may even feel like the hand is actually not a part of their body. Alien hand syndrome can sometimes lead to a person being choked, pinched, punched, undressed, and grabbed at by his or her own hand without warning while completely unaware of what his or her hand is doing until it is too late. Alien hand syndrome can occur as a result of a stroke, infection, head trauma, and tumor, and it can also be a side effect of brain surgery for severe epilepsy that requires separating the two lobes of the brain. The plus side of alien hand syndrome: you always have a worthy opponent to arm wrestle.

Read That Palm!

Many believe that the lines in your palm can actually tell quite a bit about your state of health. This ideology is based on Chinese medicine, and those who believe that palm lines can determine what illnesses you have, believe that the lines in your palms are not randomly scattered about but rather have very distinct meanings. It is believed that the palm has a combination of fourteen lines and eight types of textures that correspond to organs in the body. From your palms, you may be able to tell the condition of your kidney, liver, respiratory system, brain, and heart, as well as identify chronic respiratory diseases and blood vessel and heart diseases. Judging on how the lines of your palm look, you may want to give everyone around you high-fives, or you may start wearing gloves more often . . .

CHAPTER 14

Fingers

Do you ever have trouble putting your finger on just what's wrong with you? Whether you have deformities, swelling, blisters, bleeding, different colors, abnormally round fingernails—you name it, you'll find it discussed in this chapter. No longer will you have to bite your nails for fear of the unknown. Now you can point a finger at those people who told you that you were crazy for thinking there was something wrong with your fingers! So get reading, start biting, and put those fingers to good use—all you have to do is turn the page.

IF YOUR FINGER(S) . . .

. . . are disproportionately long

You might have an inherited disorder known as Marfan syndrome. This condition affects your body's connective tissue (the tissue responsible for anchoring and supporting your organs and strengthening structures) and causes an overgrowth of the long bones in the body. As a result, people who have Marfan syndrome are usually very thin and tall, and have fingers, toes, arms, and legs that are disproportionately long (when a person with Marfan syndrome stretches his or her arms out, for example, the length of the arm span may be longer than the person's height). Marfan syndrome can affect just about any part of the body and can cause cardiovascular problems, eye complications, and lung complications. Basically, people with Marfan syndrome are like real-life Stretch Armstrongs! Too bad they have to live with the constant threat of aneurisms, collapsed lungs, cataracts, glaucoma, emphysema, and malformed heart valves . . . Bummer!

> Marfan syndrome causes an overgrowth of the long bones in the body.

. . . is bent downward at the middle joint and your fingertip is bent back

This is known as the boutonniere deformity (or as they say in English, the buttonhole deformity). Generally speaking, this deformity is caused by inflammatory disorders like rheumatoid arthritis or by an injury such as a powerful hit to your finger as it is in the bent position, a severe burn, an injury to your finger's middle joint, or a cut to the central slip of the tendon on top of the finger. Symptoms of this condition include swelling at the top of the middle joint and not being able to straighten your finger from the middle joint. Applying a splint should help your finger heal and extend; however, if you leave this alone for too long, you may need surgery, and even then, your finger may be permanently deformed. How could something that sounds so cute be so bad? Let's blame the French . . .

Boutonniere deformity

Fingers as graceful as a swan . . .

A swan neck deformity, which is commonly caused by rheumatoid arthritis, occurs when the section of your finger that is closest to the knuckle and the tip of your finger bend downward, leaving the middle section pointing upward. This causes the finger to take on the shape of a swan's neck. Other causes of a swan neck deformity include not treating a mallet finger or being born with the condition, and swan neck deformities are also commonly seen in people suffering from Ehlers-Danlos syndrome. To treat the condition, you may be able to use a splint; however, surgery is usually necessary. Common symptoms of a swan neck deformity include not being able to make a fist and feeling the urge to fly south for the winter.

. . . are blue, red, or pale in color

You may have Buerger's disease, a rare disease that affects the arteries and veins of your arms and legs. In Buerger's disease, the blood vessels become swollen and inflamed and will become blocked with blood clots. These blood clots will eventually lead to destroyed skin tissue, and possibly infection or gangrene. Other symptoms of Buerger's disease include pain, ulcers, and a cold feeling in the hands, legs, and feet. Buerger's disease is rarely found in the United States and is much more common in the Far East and Middle East. Almost everyone that is diagnosed with the condition uses tobacco, and the only way to completely stop the disease is by quitting tobacco. If you do not quit, you risk having all or part of your affected limb amputated. That seems like a bigger drag than the one you'd take from your cigarette . . .

. . . are missing or you have a cleft hand, making it look like a claw

You may have what is known as a split-hand deformity, also known as ectrodactyly. This birth defect is the result of a genetic mutation that was inherited, and it generally is correlated with a mutation of the seventh chromosome with one or more central fingers missing. Split-hand deformity can be a symptom of an underlying cause such as Karsch-Neugebauer syndrome (which, along with split-hand deformity, also features the presence of cataracts and fast, involuntary movement of the eyes), Patterson-Stevenson syndrome (which features face and jaw abnormalities), and tibial aplasia (where fluid builds up in the skull, and there are shinbone abnormalities present). Split-hand deformity, while not a life-threatening condition, may cause serious frustrations for people trying to use chopsticks or when flipping someone the bird.

... have painful, fluid-filled blisters

You may have an infection of the herpes virus known as herpetic whitlow, also known as finger herpes. In order to develop herpetic whitlow, you must come into contact with skin that is already infected with the herpes virus (either on yourself or on someone else), and the virus has to enter the finger (which it does through a break in the skin, such as a torn cuticle). The herpes simplex virus type 1, which usually occurs on the lips, mouth, face, and nose, is responsible for 60 percent of herpetic whitlow infections, and the herpes simplex virus type 2, which occurs on the genitals and buttocks, is responsible for 40 percent of herpetic whitlow infections. If you contact herpetic whitlow from yourself (in what is known as autoinoculation), then this means that you are also carrying either herpes simplex virus type 1 or herpes simplex virus type 2. So if you start having fluid-filled blisters and you know that your hands haven't touched anyone else's sores lately . . . make sure you keep it that way.

... are swollen and have small, red, itchy areas

You may have chilblains, a painful inflammation of the small blood vessels in your skin. Chilblains occurs when your body is very cold and is then suddenly exposed to much warmer temperatures (such as warming your cold hands by a fire). The rapid heating makes the small blood vessels expand faster than the larger blood vessels can handle, and as a result, blood begins to leak into the neighboring tissue. Chilblains can lead to a very painful swelling, itching, and blistering of the skin, and usually the extremities such as the fingers, toes, nose, and ears are affected. Women, those who are underweight, and people with poor circulation have a greater chance of getting chilblains, and it occurs most often between the months of November to April, and—rather surprisingly—in areas that have high humidity and low temperatures (due to the fact that people who live in colder and dryer conditions have much warmer clothing and are better prepared for the cold). Getting cozy by the fire never sounded so . . . unpleasant.

. . . have horizontal indentations that span across your fingernails

You may have Beau's lines, which can appear in the fingernails and toenails and are the result of an injury, an illness, or may even be a sign that you are malnourished. Diseases associated with the appearance of Beau's lines include circulatory diseases (like peripheral artery disease), uncontrolled diabetes (where the disease is either not treated or not treated well enough), or illnesses that feature a high fever (such as the measles, mumps, pneumonia, or scarlet fever). As your nail grows, the Beau's lines will gradually disappear as they grow out. If you have Beau's lines on more than one finger, this may be the result of a systemic cause, such as a side effect of a particular medication—or some hard-core nail biting.

. . . have thick and abnormally rounded fingernails

This is a condition known as finger clubbing. Though the cause remains unknown, it is believed to be the result of fluid accumulation at the ends of the fingers. Finger clubbing is a common symptom of gastrointestinal disorders (such as celiac disease, liver disease, and Crohn's disease), congenital heart disease, and respiratory diseases (such as chronic obstructive pulmonary disease, cystic fibrosis, and lung cancer). Finger clubbing has also been related to Graves' disease and Hodgkin's lymphoma. There are several stages of finger clubbing. First, the skin next to the nail bed becomes shiny and the nail bed becomes soft. The nails will then curve in what is known as Scarmouth's sign. The end of the finger will then start to become larger (this is known as drumstick fingers). Though unsightly, having drumstick fingers does make Thanksgiving preparations a whole lot easier. Just take your hands out of your pockets and pass the gravy.

The end of the finger will then start to become larger (this is known as drumstick fingers).

... are pale or a grayish yellow

It's time to get out of the cold, because you may have frostbite. Frostbite is when your skin and the tissues beneath your skin begin to freeze. There are three stages of frostbite: frostnip (this is when the frostbite is mild, your skin will turn red and feel cold, you may experience a numbing or prickling sensation, and no permanent damage is done), superficial frostbite (when your red skin now turns pale, there is a chance that ice crystals are forming in your tissue, your skin feels deceptively warm, and as you warm your fingers they may seem spotty, purple, or blue and a blister will appear around a day later), and lastly, severe frostbite (where all layers of the skin are affected, your muscles and joints do not work, large blisters appear a day or two after warming, and the entire area turns hard and black due to death of the tissue). So remember to bundle up this coming winter, or ol' Jack Frost will turn that mani-pedi into a mani-deadi.

. . . is stuck in a bent position

You may have a painful condition called stenosing tenosynovitis, otherwise known as trigger finger. Trigger finger causes your finger to become stuck in a bent position and then, when you try to move the finger, it snaps back to normal, much like a trigger that is pulled and then released. Trigger finger is the result of the sheath that surrounds your finger's flexor tendon on the palm side becoming narrower due to forceful and repetitive use of that finger, and it is more common in women and those with diabetes. In severe cases of the condition, your finger may lock in the bent position. Other symptoms of trigger finger include a nodule or bump at the base of the finger, finger stiffness in the morning, and a clicking or popping sensation when moving the finger. It is usually the dominant hand that is affected by trigger finger, and it is commonly the middle finger, ring finger, or thumb that are affected, though both hands and more than one finger can have it. So the next time someone tells you that he has an itchy trigger finger, it may not be far from the truth.

. . . are bleeding under the fingernails

You may be experiencing a splinter hemorrhage. Splinter hemorrhages appear as thin lines of blood that travel the length of the nail (and make it look as though you have a splinter in your nail . . . get it?). Splinter hemorrhages can be caused by a trauma to the nail; however, if you are experiencing a splinter hemorrhage and have not recently injured your fingernail or toenail, you may be experiencing fungal nail infections, lupus, Raynaud's disease, endocarditis (which is an infection of the lining of the heart), vasculitis (where your blood vessels in the skin become inflamed and damaged), or microemboli (where there are microscopic blood clots in the bloodstream that lead to damage of the small capillaries). If you experience enough splinter hemorrhages, you'll never have to worry about buying nail polish again—assuming bloody-brown is your color.

Don't paint your fingernails just yet . . .

Those nails might actually be helpful in diagnosing your problems. According to ayurvedic medicine, nails are the waste product of your bones. If your nails break easily and are rough, dry, and crooked, this can mean you have a Vata constitution (people who move fast, think quickly, are thin, and light sleepers). If your nails appear pink, soft, are tender, and bend easily, this means you have a Pitta constitution (someone who has oily skin, is sharp, and has a fiery personality). If your nails are strong, thick, shiny, and soft, this means you have a Kapha constitution (someone who is easygoing, affectionate, graceful, and slow moving and speaking). If your nails have longitudinal lines, this could be a sign of malabsorption in your digestive system. If your nails have diagonal grooves, this could mean malnutrition or a long-standing illness. If your nails are yellow, this could mean you have jaundice or a delicate liver. If your nails are blue, this means you have a weak heart. If your nails have white splotches on them, this means that lady really screwed up your French manicure. Go back and get a refund.

CHAPTER 15

Chest

Do you have something that you need to get off your chest? Like, literally *something* you need to *get off* your chest? Perhaps you are wondering why your chest suddenly looks like a wine barrel? Or why you have a giant dent in your torso? Well, you're in the right chapter. Here you'll find the answers you need for you to come to grips with what's going on with your chest. Keep your shirt on? I don't think so!

IF YOUR CHEST . . .

. . . has a dent and looks like it is caving in

You may have a condition known as pectus excavatum where the chest bows inward and the breastbone is sunken into the chest. Pectus excavatum can become more serious as a person grows older, and a severe case can lead to the breastbone compressing the lungs and heart. This not only reduces the amount of space the lungs have to expand, but it also pushes the heart further to the left side of the chest, reducing the heart's ability to pump adequately. Often, pectus excavatum occurs in conjunction with other conditions such as scoliosis, Marfan syndrome, and mitral valve prolapse. While it can be serious, there is no denying that pectus excavatum has its perks. For example, let's say you're at a party and the host runs out of clean dishes. No plates, no problem! You have a built-in bowl for chips and dip! Just stay away from anything hot . . .

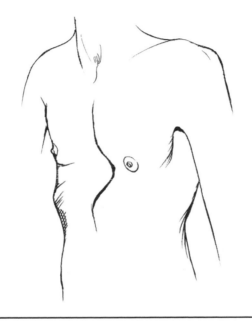

Pectus excavatum

. . . protrudes

You may have pectus carinatum, also known as "pigeon chest," a name given to the condition because of the birdlike appearance your chest has (the sternum protrudes, and there is a depression on the sides of your chest, making your chest look bowed-out, like that of a pigeon). Much like pectus excavatum (see previous entry), pectus carinatum worsens during growth spurts of late adolescence. Pectus carinatum can simply be an abnormality, or it can be a sign of other conditions such as Marfan syndrome, homocystinuria, or Morquio syndrome. Generally speaking, pectus carinatum does not affect the lungs and heart, though there are abnormalities and excessive growth of cartilage of the breastbone and ribs. In children under eighteen, a brace and a handful of breadcrumbs can be used to treat the condition (just don't give them too many or they'll never leave you alone).

. . . is round and bulging

This is known as barrel chest (due to the fact that it resembles, you guessed it, a barrel). This, in and of itself, is not a disease; this condition is caused by the overinflation of the lungs over a long period of time, which in turn makes the rib cage remain partially expanded. It also exacerbates any shortness of breath and can make you breathe less efficiently. Often, people who have chronic obstructive pulmonary disease (COPD), like emphysema, and people who have osteoarthritis and cystic fibrosis experience barrel chest. Barrel chest has also been linked to simply getting older and is seen in the elderly. So,

> Barrel chest is caused by the overinflation of the lungs over a long period of time . . .

just like how barrels are part of the aging process of alcohol, barrel chest is often a part of the aging process of people. If you open these barrels up, however, I guarantee you won't want to drink any of what's inside.

. . . has hives and your throat feels swollen

You should get yourself to the hospital right away (like, immediately) because you're most likely having an allergic reaction known as anaphylaxis. This can be fatal, and it occurs seconds or minutes after being exposed to the allergen. During anaphylaxis, your body goes into shock. Blood pressure drops quickly and the airways become more narrow, making it much more difficult to breathe normally. To immediately treat anaphylaxis, you need an injection of epinephrine. Common allergens that cause anaphylaxis include peanuts, tree nuts, shellfish, eggs, milk, and stings from bees, hornets, wasps, yellow jackets, and fire ants. Other symptoms include feeling like you have a lump in your throat, having a swollen tongue, feeling warm, wheezing, having a fast pulse, and a sense of impending doom . . . great, I think I might be having an allergic reaction to life.

. . . has small, glistening bumps

You may have a rare skin condition known as lichen nitidus. Lichen nitidus usually affects young adults and children and is the result of an abnormal inflammation of the skin cells. The glistening bumps associated with the condition appear in clusters, are usually the color of a person's skin, and are rarely itchy. The most common areas of the body where these bumps might occur are the chest, abdomen, arms, and genitals. Lichen nitidus is not contagious, is not a form of cancer, and does not increase the risk of developing skin cancer; however, it has been found to be associated with Crohn's disease, tuberculosis, juvenile rheumatoid arthritis, and eczema. At most, you may just look like you constantly have beads of sweat on your body that don't move, so if you don't want to explain your condition every time you enter a room, just pretend that you're out of breath and make up an excuse for why you had to run over there.

A broken heart can be more than just emotional . . .

Broken heart syndrome (yes, that's what it's really called) is a heart condition that is the result of stressful situations such as a breakup or the death of a loved one. Symptoms of broken heart syndrome include chest pain, an irregular heartbeat, weakness, and shortness of breath, and many people believe they are actually suffering from a heart attack. When a person has broken heart syndrome, a portion of his or her heart enlarges temporarily, leading it to not pump as efficiently, as the remaining parts of the heart act normal or have contractions that are more forceful. Broken heart syndrome is found more often in women over the age of fifty. The condition is believed to be due to a rush of stress hormones that can damage the heart temporarily. While most cases reverse in a week, broken heart syndrome has been known to be fatal. Gives a whole new meaning to the term "lady killers," doesn't it?

CHAPTER 16

Breasts

Ladies, take off your tops, because it's time to take a look at the girls. But we're not talking Mardi Gras beads and *Girls Gone Wild*. Instead, it's time to talk about what's really going on in that bra of yours. And fellas, don't feel left out; you'll be kept abreast of any ailments and illnesses that you may suffer from as well. Do you have lumps? Discharge? Crusty nipples? A uni-boob? In this chapter you'll learn what your symptoms really mean so the only question that will remain unsolved is how to fix your unsightly tan line.

IF YOUR BREASTS (FEMALE) . . .

. . . have a lump

This can be a sign of breast cancer, cysts, or fibrocystic breast condition. Fibrocystic breasts have benign lumps (there can be many) that may cause discomfort, but the condition is harmless. The lumps caused by fibrocystic breast condition are moveable and feel rubbery, and, in fact, 60 percent of women who have lumps in their breasts have this condition. Cysts are lumps that are tender and fluid-filled. If you have a new lump in your breast and are experiencing pain, swelling, nipple discharge, and redness of the nipple, you might have breast cancer. The lumps found in breast cancer are usually hard, firm, and not easy to move. If you have lumps in one or both of your breasts, you should have them checked out around a week after the start of your period. The worst-case scenario: you have cancer. The best-case scenario: Uh, do I really have to say it? You don't have cancer! Come on, I really thought that was obvious.

Take Care of Your Ta-Tas

In ayurvedic medicine, caring for the breasts is related to having a balanced Kapha, where you have nourishment, stability, and fat; if you have an unbalanced Kapha, you have a chance of tumors and stagnation. In ayurveda, it is advised to massage the breasts daily to keep them healthy. Just take ¼ teaspoon of almond oil, sesame oil, or coconut oil, and massage in a circular motion with the flat part of your fingers from the lower, outer region, across the bottom, and then move up and outward toward the underarm. Doing this massage will also reduce congestion and cysts that occur from fibrocystic breast disease. The last and most important part about ayurvedic breast care is that you have to love your breasts and accept them for what they are. And if you need help with any of this, I'm sure your husband would be glad to help.

. . . are tender and your areolas are darker than usual

You might be pregnant (though dark areolas can also be a sign of a hormonal imbalance). In the first few weeks, there are certain symptoms that are definitive for pregnancy. These symptoms include *very* tender breasts (more tender than they are before your period), darker and wider areolas (due to pregnancy hormones), an enlargement or increased amount of the little bumps found on your areola (known as Montgomery's tubercles), fatigue, nausea (as well as vomiting), spotting, bloating, an increased sensitivity to smells and odors, craving certain foods while avoiding other foods, and the ever popular frequent urination. Of course, don't just rely on this list of symptoms if you think you might be pregnant. All of these can be the result of other, completely unrelated causes. So if you find yourself experiencing these symptoms, go to the store and get yourself a pregnancy test to be sure. With the frequent urination, you'll know your results in no time!

Dark areolas can also be a sign of a hormonal imbalance.

. . . are connected together or webbed

This is known as symmastia, though it is also commonly known as "breadloafing" or as having a "uniboob." This can occur due to a rare congenital deformity of the breast, which requires plastic surgery to fix, or it can be a side effect of breast augmentation surgery. During a breast implant operation, in order for the implants to get closer to create cleavage, soft tissue that covers the breastbone or sternum is removed. If the implants sit too close to the middle of the chest, it can give a webbed appearance. Symmastia does not occur immediately following breast implant surgery, however, and it usually takes months to become noticeable. To correct symmastia, a surgical procedure known as breast revision is required to close the space in the middle of the chest. Having a uniboob does have its, well, *perks*. Think about how much money you'll save at Victoria's Secret by only having to buy one cup!

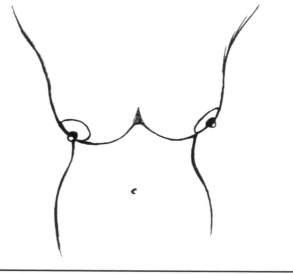

Symmastia

... have a black, green, or dirty white discharge

You may have mammary duct ectasia. This condition usually happens to women in their forties and fifties, and it involves the walls of the milk ducts thickening and filling with fluid as a result of the duct dilating and becoming inflamed. The duct can then become clogged or blocked with a sticky and thick substance. Besides nipple discharge in one or both of the breasts, other symptoms of mammary duct ectasia include tenderness of the breast—especially around the nipple—redness of the breast, a lump on the breast, and an inverted nipple. While mammary duct ectasia sounds frightening, it is in no way a sign of breast cancer, nor does it put you at greater risk of getting breast cancer. While the symptoms will go away on their own without any treatment, the memories you'll have of seeing black discharge come out of your nipple will last a lifetime.

... have oozing, crusty, flaking, and scaly skin around the nipple

You may have Paget's disease of the breast. This is a rare type of breast cancer that begins at the nipple and extends to the areola. Paget's disease of the breast can sometimes be mistaken for dermatitis or other benign skin conditions. Other symptoms of the disease include a lump in the breast, hardened skin around the nipple, redness, itching, bloody or straw-colored discharge from the nipple, a nipple that is turned-in or flat, or thick-feeling skin around the breast. Usually, only one breast is affected, and most often, women over the age of fifty are diagnosed with the disease. The changes to the skin may fluctuate in the beginning, misleading a person to believe that she is actually healing. Talk about a not-so-funny practical joke!

... have a milky discharge and you're not pregnant

This can be a sign of prolactinoma. While both men and women can be affected by prolactinoma, women are five times as likely to get it than men, and women tend to notice symptoms earlier than men. Prolactinoma occurs when the hormone prolactin is overproduced as a result of a noncancerous tumor that forms in the pituitary gland of the brain. The increase of prolactin decreases the levels of sex hormones (estrogen for women and testosterone for men) and can cause infertility, impaired vision, less interest in sexual activity, low bone density, and headaches. For women, other symptoms include not having your period, having irregular periods (which result in the earlier diagnoses), and vaginal dryness that can lead to pain while having sex. So it seems that, even when it comes to illnesses, women are more perceptive than men? Whatever. Guys still aren't going to stop and ask for directions.

... are swollen and red

You may have an infection known as mastitis. This condition is more common in women who are breast-feeding and occurs when bacteria from the mouth of the baby or the skin of your breast enter the breast through cracks or breaks in the skin of the nipple. The bacteria then enter the milk ducts and begin multiplying, resulting in an infection. Other symptoms of mastitis include tenderness of the breast, a burning sensation or pain that can be incessant or can only occur while breast-feeding, generally feeling ill, having a fever and chills, and the breast being warm to the touch. In rare occasions, mastitis occurs in women who are not lactating. If not treated properly, mastitis can lead to an abscess of the breast, milk stasis (when milk is not drained completely from the breast and inflammation occurs due to increased pressure on the ducts and milk leaking into breast tissue), and a recurrence of the infection. Treatment of mastitis includes frequent feeding or pumping the breasts, alternating hot and cold compresses, taking antibiotics,

In rare occasions, mastitis occurs in women who are not lactating.

adjusting the way you breast-feed, and never forgiving your child for making your breast blow up like a balloon so he or she could have a snack.

IF YOUR BREASTS (MALE) . . .

. . . have a lump

Does this sound familiar? Don't think just because you're a man you can't also have breast cancer. Both men and women are born with breast tissue that is made up of lobules (milk-producing glands). During puberty, women develop *more* breast tissue, but men do still have a small portion of it, and even that small portion can host cancerous cells. Symptoms of male breast cancer include a painless lump in the breast or a thickening of breast tissue; skin changes such as puckering, dimpling, scaling, and redness; nipple changes like scaling, redness, and your nipple turning inward; and discharge coming from your nipple. Male breast cancer is usually found in older men, and if diagnosed early, there is a good chance that you will go into remission with surgery and/or chemotherapy. So remember fellas, women's breasts aren't the only ones you should be paying attention to.

. . . are enlarged

You may have gynecomastia, a swelling of the male breast tissue caused by an imbalance of estrogen and testosterone (you are either producing too much estrogen or not enough testosterone) or by certain drugs, like Flagyl or Tagamet. Symptoms of gynecomastia include enlarged, swollen, and sometimes tender breasts, and one or both of your breasts can be affected. Gynecomastia can be caused by many different conditions that throw off the body's balance of hormones, including kidney failure, hypogonadism (which interferes with production of testosterone), hyperthyroidism, cirrhosis and liver failure, tumors, and even starvation and malnutrition. While gynecomastia is most prevalent for males between fifty and eighty years old, it can occur during puberty, and more than 50 percent of all male babies are born with gynecomastia. Gynecomastia usually disappears on its own over time, so calm down, invest in a good sports bra, and stop being such a girl about it.

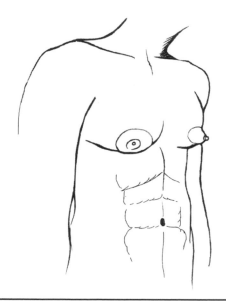

Gynecomastia

. . . are underdeveloped or absent on one side

You may have Poland syndrome, which is usually present at birth and consists of malformations on one side of the body (the right side of the body is twice as likely to be affected than the left side). Other than the underdeveloped breast, you may also notice an absence or underdevelopment of the nipple, an underdeveloped hand or arm, a lack of armpit hair on the affected arm, and very short, webbed fingers. Poland syndrome is more likely to occur in males than females and, in mild cases of Poland syndrome, the malformation to the breast might not occur until a person is older. It is estimated that one in every 30,000 people has Poland syndrome. It is important to note that the underdevelopment caused by Poland syndrome is unrelated to the underdevelopment caused by the communist regime that once ruled Poland. But let's blame the commies anyway. Those webbed-fingered, single-breasted bastards!

. . . have red, sore, and irritated nipples

You need to reconsider what you're wearing on those early morning runs, because you may have jogger's nipple, an irritation of the nipple that can lead to cracking and bleeding that occurs as a result of your clothing rubbing and chafing your nipple (or nipples). Jogger's nipple is most commonly seen in runners (hence the name), though it can happen to anyone, and erect nipples are more prone to the condition. Jogger's nipple is more common in men who wear tight-fitting tops or shirts made of coarse material like cotton and in women who do not wear a bra while they run. To prevent jogger's nipple, you can place surgical tape over your nipple, wear shirts made of silk fabric or Lycra, or if you're a woman, you should wear a supportive bra while exercising. To soothe the irritation, you should use coconut oil, petroleum jelly, or a lanolin cream. Men can also avoid jogger's nipple by running without a shirt on, and women . . . should too . . .

CHAPTER 17

Stomach

Sometimes, knowing that something is wrong with you can be hard to stomach. Whether you're swollen or extremely thin, you have good reason to be concerned because stomach issues can be pretty unsettling. Whether you're facing inflammatory bowel disease, celiac disease, cancer, and even tapeworm, your stomach can—and will—let you know when something is not right. So take a moment to swallow those butterflies, look into your symptoms, and digest the information. You'll be glad you did.

IF YOUR STOMACH . . .

. . . is swollen and you are severely constipated

You may have a very serious disorder known as intussusception where the colon or the small intestine slides into another area of the intestine, forming a blockage and preventing any fluid or food from passing through. In children, intussusception is the most common cause of intestinal obstruction. In adults, however, intussusception is rare and could be a sign of an underlying condition. Other symptoms of intussusception include rectal bleeding, a change in the regularity of bowel movements, abdominal pain, nausea, and vomiting. Adults who have the condition may also have malignant or benign growths, adhesions in their intestines, irritable bowel syndrome, gastroparesis, Hirschsprung's disease, or chronic diarrhea. It's a good thing intussusception doesn't cause a lisp; no one would ever be able to tell their friends what they're suffering from.

> Other symptoms of intussusception include rectal bleeding . . .

. . . is swollen or distended

This can be a sign of many conditions, including irritable bowel syndrome, lactose intolerance, an ovarian cyst, uterine fibroids, a buildup of fluid, food poisoning, a tumor, heart failure, advanced stages of cancer, parasites, and, of course, having gas and overeating. While abdominal swelling is not always serious, if symptoms such as difficulty breathing, shock, severe pain, or bowel obstruction occur, it can be a sign of a life-threatening condition. Other symptoms of a swollen stomach include not being able to fit into your jeans and having to resort to sweat pants, turning "just one more" cookie into seven or eight cookies, and losing all dignity and self-respect when chocolate and peanut butter are combined.

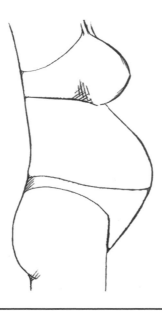

Lactose intolerance

You might not expect some of these foods to leave you feeling bloated . . .

Broccoli, cauliflower, cabbage, Brussels sprouts, peppers, onions, and citrus fruits all create more gas in your GI tract, which can lead to bloating. Drinks that are high in acid, such as coffee, tea, alcohol, and acidic fruit juices, can also cause swelling because they irritate the GI tract. Fried foods will bloat you and make you feel heavy due to the fact that they are digested more slowly. Even chewing gum can bloat you because as you chew, you swallow air, which becomes trapped in the GI tract. So the next time someone tells you to eat your vegetables, tell them you can't because you're watching your figure.

... is swollen and you have yellow skin

You may have a rare liver disease known as hepatic vein obstruction, otherwise known as Budd-Chiari syndrome. The hepatic vein carries the blood out of the liver, and when it becomes blocked from either clotting or a tumorous growth, the blood cannot be returned to the heart. In some occasions, blockages can be broken up with the aid of anticlotting medications, but most of the time, surgery is needed to unblock the obstructed veins. Most people who suffer from Budd-Chiari syndrome also suffer from some underlying condition that is responsible for the blood clotting; however, the condition can also occur as a result of pregnancy or use of oral contraceptives. Other symptoms of Budd-Chiari syndrome include vomiting blood or pain on the right side of the upper abdomen. Nothing scary about that, right!

> Most of the time, surgery is needed to unblock the obstructed veins.

... is swollen and you have diarrhea, a fever, and are vomiting

You might have a stomach flu, also known as gastroenteritis. Gastroenteritis is actually not the flu at all but rather an inflammation and irritation of the intestines and stomach. While the most common cause of gastroenteritis is a virus, it can also be caused by certain food-borne illnesses like salmonella, campylobacter, and shigella; bacteria like *E. coli*; and parasites like giardia or cryptosporidium. Other symptoms include abdominal cramps, nausea, headaches, and muscle aches. When gastroenteritis is caused by a virus, it usually lasts only one to two days. When caused by another agent, however, the symptoms can last for a much longer period of time (sometimes, longer than two weeks!). Half of the cases of gastroenteritis in adults are caused by a norovirus, which is highly contagious and can spread very quickly. Norovirus: the gift that keeps on giving!

Do you have a hard, red lump in your belly button?

Stop praying for it to go away and get yourself to a doctor! You likely have a Sister Mary Joseph nodule, a tumor that is often associated with an advanced stage of stomach, pancreatic, or ovarian cancer. Sister Mary Joseph was a Catholic nurse who worked with the Mayo brothers (who would later go on to create the Mayo Clinic); she noticed that patients with terminal carcinoma would sometimes develop red, swollen lesions in their belly button. While the prognosis is poor for someone who has a Sister Mary Joseph nodule due to the fact that there is usually metastasis found in other parts of the abdomen and body, there is some good news. In 15 percent of patients with a Sister Mary Joseph nodule, no primary cancer is found. On second thought, maybe a little praying won't hurt. But get yourself checked out first.

. . . is extremely thin

This can be the result of several different conditions. Most likely, extreme thinness is caused by malnutrition, eating disorders like anorexia or bulimia, and excessive dieting and exercise, but it can also be the result of certain illnesses such as cancer, AIDS, hyperthyroidism, depression, and Crohn's disease, a type of inflammatory bowel disease that usually creates chronic inflammation of the gastrointestinal tract anywhere from the mouth to the anus. Other symptoms of Crohn's disease include watery diarrhea, cramps and abdominal pain, and pain when passing stool. The disease usually occurs between the ages of fifteen and thirty-five, and those that smoke, have a history of the disease in their family, or are of Jewish ancestry are at the greatest risk of having the illness. For some people, being thin is a lifelong goal, but when it goes too far it can be a real pain in the rear.

> The disease usually occurs between the ages of fifteen and thirty-five . . .

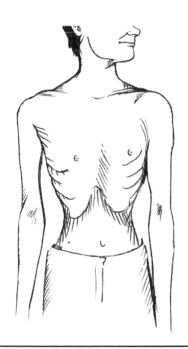

Malnutrition

. . . is very thin and you are experiencing abdominal discomfort

You may have a genetic digestive condition known as celiac disease. People with celiac disease are not allowed to eat bread, cookies, pasta, or anything else containing rye, wheat, or barley, because they have an adverse reaction to gluten, a protein that is found in all of these foods.

When a person with celiac disease eats something containing gluten, the villi, which line the intestines and help in the process of absorbing nutrients, become damaged. As a result, the body is not able to absorb the nutrients sufficiently, and the individual can become malnourished. This can eventually lead to deprivation of essential vitamins for the brain, bones, peripheral nervous system, liver, and other organs in the body. The exact cause of celiac disease is unknown, and a person can develop the disease at any time. Symptoms vary widely from person to person, making the condition sometimes hard to diagnose, though many people complain of diarrhea, bloating, abdominal pain, and lactose intolerance. So if you start noticing that you haven't been gaining any weight from your nightly milk and cookies, maybe it's because you shouldn't be eating milk or cookies in the first place . . . Or maybe you're just lucky.

> People with celiac disease are not allowed to eat bread, cookies, pasta, or anything else containing rye, wheat, or barley . . .

(Don't) Do the Worm

Another reason you might be losing weight might be because you have a parasitic tapeworm inside of your body that is stealing your nutrients. In an invasive tapeworm infection, which can be caused by consuming water or food that is contaminated with tapeworm eggs, the eggs migrate outside of the intestines and form cysts on your tissues and organs (this can eventually lead to seizures if they reach the brain). In an intestinal tapeworm infection, tapeworm larvae are consumed and become adults that live in your intestines. Not only can the adult tapeworm live for twenty years, but it can measure up to fifty feet long! Once the tapeworm adheres to the walls of your intestine, it will also begin to produce eggs. Symptoms of an intestinal tapeworm infection include weight loss, abdominal pain, nausea, weakness, and a loss of appetite. The most common way to get a tapeworm is by eating raw or undercooked meat (such as pork, beef, and fish) that came from an infected animal. Now, if you'll excuse me, I'm going to go throw up.

CHAPTER 18

Pelvis

Do you have varicose veins? Is one leg shorter than the other? Are your hips swollen? Do you have an unusual amount of vaginal discharge? It's time to get hip to what your body is telling you. Pops, snaps, limps: These aren't new dance moves, these are signs that your pelvis, genitals, and hips have problems that need to be addressed. Admitting that you have pelvis and hip problems might make you sound old, and admitting that you have some problems down there might make you feel kind of sad, but you know what? Now you get to ride those scooters in the supermarket. And watch discounted movies. And take out your teeth. Where can we sign up?

IF YOUR PELVIS . . .

. . . has a lump

This can be a sign of several things, including a cyst; testicular cancer; sexually transmitted diseases like chlamydia, gonorrhea, or genital herpes; and a hernia. Hernias are created when soft tissue protrudes through tears or weak spots of the lower abdominal wall. When found in the pelvic region they are known as inguinal hernias and are more commonly found in men. These bulges are painful, particularly when lifting heavy objects, coughing, or bending over. Inguinal hernias do not get better over time, and if untreated, they can potentially be life-threatening. Hernias enlarge, putting pressure on the surrounding tissues (which, for men, can lead to swelling of the scrotum—and not the good kind, if you catch my drift), and can become incarcerated hernias (when a loop of your intestine gets trapped and obstructs your bowel). They can also strangulate, which is when a part of the intestine gets trapped, diminishing blood flow of this intestine and possibly leading to death of the tissue; strangulation is life-threatening and should be treated immediately. Incarcerate, strangulation, pain after bending over, and heavy lifting . . . hernias are like the original "don't drop the soap" joke.

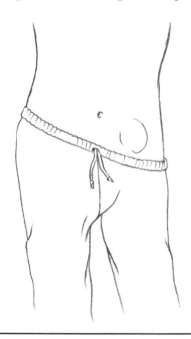

Hernia

... has varicose veins

If you're a woman, you may have a condition known as pelvic congestion syndrome. These varicose veins tend to develop when you are pregnant and continue to progress afterward. Though it is unknown why these varicose veins form, there are several theories. One possible cause of pelvic congestion syndrome is that the excess fluid and weight gain associated with pregnancy causes your veins to swell, and over time, your veins become distended because the valves in the veins are damaged. Another theory is that the walls of your veins weaken due to the high amounts of estrogen while pregnant (which would explain why men don't get pelvic congestion syndrome). The last theory is that being pregnant may actually change the anatomy of your veins, making them more susceptible to damage. Unfortunately, scientists have not researched the theory that your unborn child may be planting microscopic bombs inside of your veins as a form of premature payback for the emotional damage that you will undoubtedly cause him or her down the road. But they should really get on that; it's as good a reason as any . . .

... hurts and you have unusually heavy vaginal discharge

You may have pelvic inflammatory disease, or PID, which is actually a generic term for a group of conditions that affect the female reproductive organs (sorry fellas, you're going to have to sit this one out). The conditions that make up pelvic inflammatory disease include cervicitis (an inflammation of the cervix), endometritis (an inflammation of the uterine lining), salpingitis (an inflammation of the fallopian tubes), and peritonitis (an inflammation of the membrane that covers the abdominal organs and lines the abdominal cavity). Other symptoms of PID include back pain, uterine bleeding that seems abnormal, pain while urinating, and pain while having sex. PID is most commonly caused by *Neisseria gonorrhoeae*, the bacteria that causes gonorrhea, and *Chlamydia trachomatis*, the bacteria that causes chlamydia. This group of conditions is like a veritable buffet of vaginal inflammation, but you probably won't want to go back for seconds.

Men, if you have discomfort in your pelvis . . .

You may have prostate cancer. There aren't usually any symptoms of prostate cancer early on, so if you are experiencing pelvic discomfort, have trouble urinating, or have less powerful urinations, blood in your semen, or swollen legs, you should see a doctor immediately because these are signs of advanced stages of the condition. Prostate cancer is actually one of the most common types of cancer that affects men, and the risk of developing the disease increases as you grow older (it is most often seen in men older than the age of sixty-four). Other risk factors for developing prostate cancer include having a history of prostate cancer in your family, being obese, and being of African descent. So if you are experiencing discomfort in your pelvis, speak up before you get too old. If you don't, you might not have the chance . . .

. . . has dark red, pus-filled bumps that itch

It's time to get out of the hot tub, because you may have pseudomonas folliculitis, also known as hot tub folliculitis. *Pseudomonas aeruginosa* is a bacteria that lives in wet and warm environments, and there is no better environment for it to thrive than in hot tubs (especially those made from wood). This bacteria leads to an infection of the hair follicles, and symptoms can occur within hours of contact. The resulting rash may be thicker where you wear your bathing suit due to the fact that the material of your bathing suit holds the contaminated water, allowing for the bacteria to remain in contact with your skin for a longer amount of time. A surefire way to see if you have hot tub folliculitis? See if everyone else that was in the hot tub has it, too. The most common way to get pseudomonas folliculitis? Appear on *The Jersey Shore*.

> The resulting rash may be thicker where you wear your bathing suit . . .

IF YOUR GENITALS (MALE) . . .

. . . have a white, yellow, or green discharge

Give yourself a round of applause, because you, my friend, might have gonorrhea, otherwise known as "the clap." Gonorrhea is a sexually transmitted disease that is caused by bacteria, and it can be spread to the mouth, penis, vagina, and anus. Other symptoms of gonorrhea for men include swollen or tender testicles, a swollen or red urethra, a burning sensation while peeing, a sore throat, and more frequent urination (and it should be noted that a cloudy discharge is a sign of chlamydia). The symptoms of gonorrhea usually take up to a week to appear after you're exposed; however, sometimes in men it can take as long as a month. You can catch gonorrhea by having sex with someone who is already infected. The good news is that gonorrhea can easily be treated with antibiotics. So luckily for you, it's clap on, clap off.

... have a hard lump or scar tissue that causes your penis to bend

You may have Peyronie's disease. The lump develops in the layers where the erectile tissue is, and the result can be a curved and painful erection. Your penis may have a very significant curve to it (downward, upward, or to one side), and this curve may lead to erectile dysfunction and a shortening of the penis. Though the cause of Peyronie's disease is still not fully known, it is believed that the disease occurs when blood vessels in the penis rupture due to damage or athletic activity, and as the penis heals, the cells become trapped at the site of the injury and scar tissue begins to then build up. The curve of the penis occurs because, when the penis becomes erect, the scar tissue does not stretch, which makes the penis bend and become disfigured. While it can be embarrassing to have Peyronie's disease, the extra coat rack sure makes for a fun party trick.

... are inflamed at the head of your penis

You may have balanitis or balanoposthitis, an inflammation of the penis head and foreskin. Balanitis (which also includes a rash, itching, and a bad-smelling discharge) usually occurs in those who are not circumcised (much like balanoposthitis, but perhaps the swollen foreskin was a dead giveaway there) and in those who have poor hygiene. It can be caused by dermatitis or an infection brought on by not washing under the foreskin correctly. Circumcision actually prevents balanitis and bala-noposthitis from occurring because, well, if you don't have a foreskin, you don't have anything to be irritated. If the cause of your balanitis is an infection, an antifungal or antibiotic medication can be used to treat the condition. If, however, inflammation is severe and persistent, a circumcision may actually be the recommended choice of treatment. Good luck with that . . .

Some shrinkage is normal, but this is just ridiculous . . .

Usually found in Southeast Asia, China, and Africa, koro syndrome is a psychiatric disorder that occurs when a man actually believes that his penis is shrinking into his abdomen or that it has been stolen. People with koro syndrome not only fear their penis is retracting, but they believe that this will lead to death. In fact, at one point, people in Sudan believed that if they shared a comb, shook hands, or were verbally cursed at, their penises would melt away. The hysteria was so impactful that local media warned everyone traveling to Sudan to not shake hands with anyone. Imagine how everyone reacted when they got out of a cold shower . . .

. . . have a lump in either one of your testicles

You may have testicular cancer. Other symptoms of testicular cancer include feeling a sense of heaviness in your scrotum, feeling pain or discomfort in your scrotum or testicle, a collection of fluid in the scrotum that happens suddenly, a dull ache in the groin or abdomen, and tenderness or enlargement of your breasts. Testicular cancer generally only affects one testicle, and people who have had an inguinal hernia; abnormalities in the penis, testicles, or kidneys; have a history of testicular cancer; or have an undescended testicle (even if it was fixed in surgery) are at the most risk of getting the cancer. Most forms of testicular cancer begin in the germ cells, which are responsible for producing the immature sperm. While testicular cancer is rare, it is the most common cancer among American males aged fifteen to thirty-four. The easiest way to know if you have testicular cancer is to perform self-examinations. And let's face it: Between the ages of fifteen and thirty-four, your hands are always down there anyway, so why not do some good while you're at it?

... have a single round, painless, open sore

This is usually a sign of a bacteria-related STD known as syphilis. There are three stages to syphilis: the primary stage, where a single sore or ulcer known as a chancre appears; the secondary stage, where there is a rash, the development of warty patches, and possibly fever, swollen lymph nodes, hair loss, and muscle pain; and the tertiary, or late, stage, where all of the symptoms seemingly disappear yet the person remains infected. If the condition goes untreated, this can lead to late syphilis, which appears years later and can lead to damage of the eyes, heart, bones, central nervous system, and large blood vessels. Because the symptoms seem to go away, many people do not treat the condition, and it continues to spread through sexual activity. Syphilis can be treated with antibiotics, prevented by using a condom, and spread by a complete lack of common sense. Seriously, you had an open sore on your penis and you thought, "Gee, maybe I should wait this one out and see where it takes me?"

... itch and you have eggs or bugs on them

You may have crabs, otherwise known as pubic lice. Pubic lice are small insects that resemble sea crabs (hence the name), and they are less than three millimeters long. Much like head lice, pubic lice feed on the blood of their host, and their bites itch. The most common way to catch crabs is through sexual intercourse. There are three different stages of pubic lice: nits (which are the eggs of pubic lice and are found attached to the hair shaft), nymphs (the lice that hatch from the eggs), and the adults (which do not move as fast as head lice and typically attach to the hair). Female pubic lice are usually larger than male pubic lice and can lay up to thirty eggs (with a lifespan of less than a month, they can lay up to three eggs a day). That kind of information would put anyone in a crabby mood.

> Much like head lice, pubic lice feed on the blood of their host, and their bites itch.

. . . stay erect for more than four hours

You may be suffering from priapism. Erections from priapism are not brought on by arousal or sexual stimulation and are typically painful. There are three types of priapism: ischemic priapism (where blood isn't able to leave the penis), nonischemic priapism (where there is just too much blood flow to the penis), and a stuttering priapism (an ischemic priapism that occurs over and over again). Priapism can be caused by blood disorders like leukemia or sickle cell anemia, certain medications (such as Viagra, Cialis, Levitra, and even antidepressants like Prozac and Wellbutrin), drug and alcohol use, injury or trauma to the genitals (which causes excessive blood flow), an injury to the spinal cord, blood clots, and even as the result of poisonous venom (such as that of a scorpion or black widow spider). If you have an ischemic priapism, you should seek medical attention immediately. Priapism: the only time an erect penis and a nurse can be in the same room without it being porn . . .

...have a hard time staying erect

You may have erectile dysfunction. Symptoms of erectile dysfunction include having difficulty getting an erection, having difficulty keeping the erection, and having a lower sex drive. Erectile dysfunction can be caused by both physical and psychological factors. Stress, anxiety, your mental state, and the state of your relationship can all cause erectile dysfunction. Other common, more physical causes include heart disease, diabetes, obesity, clogged blood vessels, multiple sclerosis, and Parkinson's disease. Erectile dysfunction can lead to relationship problems, anxiety, a low self-esteem, and even the inability to have children. To treat the condition, seek medical advice to see if your erectile dysfunction is caused by an underlying problem, and then take the necessary steps. Erectile dysfunction can worsen if you smoke, are overweight, do not exercise, drink or take drugs, or are not able to work out the issues with your partner. So remember, talk it out before you whip it out.

...have swollen lymph nodes

You may have a rare sexually transmitted disease known as lymphogranuloma venereum (LGV). Three different types of the bacteria *Chlamydia trachomatis* cause LGV (these types of the bacteria are not responsible for causing chlamydia, despite its name). LGV is more commonly found in men and in people living in Central America and South America. The first sign of LGV will occur anywhere from three to thirty days following contact with the bacteria. A small, pus-filled, painless lesion or bump develops on the scrotum, penis, vulva, or vagina. Two to six weeks later, you will experience a painful swelling of the lymph nodes in the groin (or anus) that may open and start to drain. The genitals will then start to become swollen and continue to drain, and if the anus is infected, there can be scarring, abscesses, and pain while defecating. Lymphogranuloma vene-reum can be treated with antibiotics and some lessons on who you should and should not have sex with.

IF YOUR GENITALS (FEMALE) . . .

. . . have a strong-smelling and possibly white, yellow, or green discharge

You likely have gonorrhea. Symptoms of gonorrhea in women can be very mild and similar to other STDs like chlamydia, and half of the women who have gonorrhea also have chlamydia. These symptoms include a burning sensation while peeing, abnormal bleeding, more frequent urination, a sore throat, and pain while having sexual intercourse. If the infection spreads to your stomach and fallopian tubes, you will experience a great pain in your lower abdomen and have a fever. If you are preg-nant and you have gonorrhea, you can actually pass the disease on to your child during delivery or even while it is still in the womb. Gonorrhea can also lead to infertility, and if it scars your fallopian tubes, this can lead to an ectopic pregnancy (a pregnancy outside the uterus) or difficulty conceiving. So get checked out, take your antibiotics, and save the clap for when it's needed—when you're cured.

. . . have warts

You most likely have—now see if you can follow me here—genital warts. You good so far? Genital warts are actually a type of sexually transmitted infection (STI) caused by the human papillomavirus (HPV). There are over 100 different types of HPV, and HPV is the same virus that can cause cervical cancer.

Many men can have the HPV responsible for causing genital warts and never show any symptoms. This is especially troubling because they may not be aware of their condition and can unknowingly spread the virus to other women. Just because you don't see warts doesn't mean that they don't carry the virus. Genital warts appear as small bumps or can group together to look almost like cauliflower. They are itchy, create discomfort, and can bleed during sexual intercourse. Genital warts on women can grow on the vaginal walls, the vulva, the cervix, and the area between your genitals and your anus. If you're still not convinced that genital warts are bad, take a long hard look at a piece of cauliflower. Now imagine that sprouting out of your vagina. Yeah. Not so pleasant, is it?

. . . have a soft bulge protruding through the vaginal opening

You may have a rectocele. A rectocele occurs when the front wall of the rectum bulges into the vagina due to a weakened fascia, a piece of fibrous tissue that separates the rectum from the vagina. While rarely painful, a rectocele can cause discomfort. A rectocele is the result of large amounts of pressure placed on the fascia, and the most common cause is all that pressure put on these tissues during pregnancy and childbirth, which causes the fascia, muscles, and ligaments to stretch and become weakened. If you have many pregnancies, you have a greater chance of developing a rectocele. Other conditions that can cause a rectocele include being obese, repeated heavy lifting, bronchitis or having a chronic cough, and straining from bowel movements or having chronic constipation. So whether it's a child or just a bad case of number two, you better get whatever is inside of you out—and make it go as smoothly as possible.

... have a bad-smelling odor or different colored discharge

You may have an inflammation of the vagina known as vaginitis. Vaginitis is usually caused by an infection or a change of the balance of bacteria found in the vagina. The most common forms of vaginitis are yeast infections, bacterial vaginosis (where one of the organisms that is normally found in the vagina begins to overgrow), vaginal atrophy (an inflammation due to a decline of estrogen), and trichomoniasis (an STI caused by a parasite). Other symptoms of vaginitis include irritation and itching of the vagina, pain during sexual intercourse, pain while urinating, and light spotting or bleeding. If your discharge is grayish white and has a bad odor, this could be bacterial vaginosis. If your discharge is thick like cottage cheese and you are very itchy, this is most likely a yeast infection. If your discharge is greenish yellow and sometimes frothy, this indicates you are suffering from trichomoniasis. If you've read this after eating, I sincerely apologize.

... have white, wrinkled, blotchy patches

You may have a skin condition known as lichen sclerosus. While any part of the body can be affected by lichen sclerosus, usually the vulva, the foreskin, or the anus are affected, and postmenopausal women are at a greater risk of getting the disorder. The white, blotchy patches of lichen sclerosus originally start out as smooth, white dots on the skin and later turn into the wrinkled, blotchy patches. Other symptoms include itching, discomfort, tenderness, blistering, bleeding, easy tearing and bruising, and pain while having sex. Though the cause of lichen sclerosus is still unknown, it is believed to be related to an overactive immune system or a lack of sex hormones in the part of the skin that is affected. Lichen sclerosus is not contagious and it will not spread by sexual intercourse, but that won't matter much because you won't be getting much action down there once your mate gets a good look.

. . . bleed after intercourse

You may have cervical cancer. Most cases of cervical cancer are caused by the human papillomavirus (HPV), which is transmitted between sexual partners. As the virus enters a woman's body, the woman's immune system usually prevents it from causing harm to the body. For some women, however, the virus can survive for years, which contributes to the process that makes cells become cancerous. Other symptoms of cervical cancer include bleeding between periods, bleeding after menopause, having pain in your pelvis, having pain while having sex, and having bloody, watery discharge that may have a bad-smelling odor and be heavy. Cervical cancer can also lead to tumors in the vagina. Treatment for cervical cancer includes radiation, chemotherapy, and a hysterectomy (where the uterus is removed along with the cervix). An unfortunate side effect of treating cervical cancer is infertility. Another reason for bleeding after intercourse is a breaking of the hymen that occurs from the first time a woman has sex. But, if you're reading this, I can only hope that you know enough about sex to know that . . .

. . . bleed after menopause

You may have polyps, uterine cancer, an infection of the cervix or uterus, endometrial hyperplasia, or an endometrial atrophy. If you have any bleeding after menopause, it is crucial that you get yourself checked by a doctor, because any bleeding, even if it is just a little spotting, is abnormal. Endometrial hyperplasia is when the uterine lining becomes thick due to high levels of estrogen and low levels of progesterone (called estrogen dominance), and this condition can sometimes lead to endometrial cancer. Endometrial atrophy, on the other hand, is a thinning of the uterine lining due to lower levels of estrogen that occurs as a result of menopause. Bleeding after menopause can also be the result of blood-thinning medications or hormone therapy. But look on the bright side, at least you're not having your period again.

If you're bleeding in between your periods . . .

You may have cervical cancer, endometrial cancer, uterine cancer, vaginitis, or cervicitis. Cervicitis, which is inflammation of the cervix, can occur as the result of an injury to the cervix (by inserting a foreign object into the vagina), devices used for birth control (like a diaphragm or cervical cap), infection as a result of a sexually transmitted disease, forgetting to remove a tampon once your period has ended, or cancer. Oftentimes, cervicitis goes untreated because women are not aware they have the condition, which can lead to very severe consequences. If cervicitis goes untreated, it can lead to cervical cancer, pelvic inflammatory disease, chronic pelvic pain, ectopic pregnancy, infertility, and complications when delivering. More than half of all women will develop this condition at some point in their life, and it is often found in women under the age of twenty-five. So if your period seems more like a run-on sentence, go get things checked out.

. . . have painful blisters on the lips of your vagina

You may have herpes. Herpes is actually caused by two viruses: herpes simplex virus type 1 (HSV-1) and herpes simplex virus type 2 (HSV-2). Herpes simplex virus type 1 causes cold sores of the mouth and lips, while herpes simplex virus type 2 is the cause of genital herpes (though it can also be spread by the mouth). Approximately one out of every four women is infected with HSV-2, while one out of eight men are infected with it. Other symptoms of genital herpes include vaginal discharge, ulcers (caused by the blisters breaking and crusting over), feeling sick, muscle aches, and tender and enlarged lymph nodes when having an outbreak. The first outbreak will usually occur within two weeks after being infected; however, some people may not show symptoms or it may be very mild (just because there aren't any signs doesn't mean a person isn't infected). It seems like one of the little-known side effects of herpes should be paranoia . . .

. . . have a lump or sore near the vulva

You may have vulvar cancer. The vulva is the outer skin that includes the labia and clitoris and surrounds the vagina and urethra. The most common symptom of vulvar cancer is a sore or lump that causes pain or itching. Other symptoms include bleeding not due to menstruation, thickening of the skin, or a change in color of the skin. Vulvar cancer can occur at any age; however, it is more commonly found in older women. There are two types of vulvar cancer: vulvar squamous cell carcinoma (which is the most common form of vulvar cancer and begins in the cells that line the vulva's surface) and vulvar melanoma (which starts in the cells of the vulva skin that produce pigment). As if lumps or sores near the vulva weren't bad enough, now it's going to be almost impossible for your husband to find your clitoris . . .

. . . have a lump near the opening of the vagina

This may be a Bartholin cyst. The Bartholin glands, which are located on each side of the vaginal opening, secrete a fluid to lubricate the vagina. If the openings of the Bartholin glands are obstructed, fluid can back up and turn into a cyst. While a Bartholin cyst is relatively painless, it can get infected and become an abscess. Treatment varies depending on the severity of the cyst; sometimes treatment is not needed, but other times—especially when the cyst causes pain and discomfort, is infected, or becomes an abscess—it is absolutely necessary. Treatment options include sitz baths, warm compresses, surgical drainage, antibiotics, or marsupialization (a procedure similar to surgical drainage, where an incision is made on both sides of the vagina so that a catheter can be used to drain the fluid). What? Marsupialization is a perfect treatment for those problems down under.

IF YOUR HIPS . . .

. . . are swollen

This can be the result of a form of arthritis known as hip rheumatoid arthritis. This condition, which affects three times as many women as it does men, can cause a severe pain in the hip and stiffness in the lower back, groin, and thigh. Any form of rheumatoid arthritis can cause joint damage that can be permanent, and symptoms can occur gradually or come on suddenly. Exercise is very important when it comes to helping your hip rheumatoid arthritis. It not only helps you remain flexible, but it can play a key role in supporting the joints and strengthening the muscles. If your joints become destroyed or the pain is severe, hip surgery is an option to treat the condition. While hip rheumatoid arthritis may sound bad, at least it gets you to the gym.

. . . cause one leg to be shorter than the other

Though dysplasia of the hip (when the hip joint is dislocated) is commonly found in large dogs, it also affects humans. Most often, babies are affected with hip dysplasia and show the most visible symptoms (though it can also happen to older women). The cause of developmental dysplasia of the hip, or DDH, is unknown. It has been shown, however, that if during pregnancy there are low levels of amniotic fluid in the womb, this can increase a baby's risk of having the condition. The symptoms of DDH include a much wider distance between the legs, a leg that appears much shorter than the other leg, a leg that turns outward, and skin folds that appear unevenly on the buttocks or thigh. If you or your child experience symptoms of DDH but don't want to pay costly medical bills, there's always the local veterinarian . . .

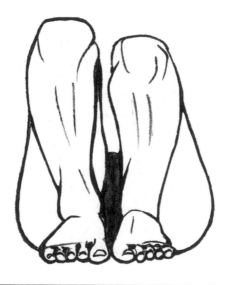

Developmental dysplasia

. . . make a popping sound and snap when extended

You may have the-ever-so-cleverly-entitled "snapping hip syndrome." There are three main causes of the condition: an iliotibial band snap, an iliopsoas tendon snap, and a hip labral tear.

In an iliotibial band snap, the iliotibial band—a thick tendon that sits over the outer area of the hip joint—snaps over the bony surface at the top of the femur, known as the greater trochanter. In an iliopsoas tendon snap, the iliopsoas tendon—the main muscle that you use to flex your hip—catches on a bony surface in the pelvis, causing it to snap as the hip is flexing. A hip labral tear, which is the least common cause of snapping hip syndrome, is when the hip joint has a tear in the cartilage. If the hip is moved while there is a loose piece of cartilage, it may catch within the joint and cause a snap. Snapping hip syndrome can be particularly useful if you want to get into playing music. Pick up your instrument, start walking, and let your natural metronome set the tempo.

... hurt and you begin walking with a limp

You may have a slipped epiphysis. This condition usually affects individuals from the ages of nine to eighteen and occurs when the head of the thigh bone, also known as the femur, slips out of its normal placement. When this occurs, either one or both of the hips can be affected, and there is pain in the hip and knee. A slipped epiphysis leads to limited joint mobility and can cause you to walk with a limp. While the cause of this condition is unknown, it occurs three times as much in men than it does in women, and it is usually a slow process that develops over time. The affected leg may appear shorter or turned outward, and a person will typically not be able to bear any weight on this leg. To treat the condition, surgery must be performed in order to prevent the femur from slipping any further. It turns out your bones can be just as clumsy as you . . .

CHAPTER 19

Buttocks

Experiencing symptoms on your buttocks can be pretty, well, crappy. But if you are experiencing bumps, blood, rashes, or worse (and *there are worse*), then you would be an ass not to make sure you were okay. Which is where this chapter of the book comes in. Here you'll learn what's wrong with your derriere before you become the butt of Mother Nature's bad joke. And if there's one thing all hypochondriacs know, it's that Mother Nature can be a real asshole. So take care of yours while you can.

IF YOUR BUTTOCKS . . .

. . . have lesions, red bumps, blackheads, painful lumps, and scarring

You may have an inflammation of the skin known as hidradenitis suppurativa, a very severe form of acne that occurs in regions where there is a large concentration of sweat glands and where your skin rubs together. Common areas where hidradenitis suppurativa occurs include the buttocks, the armpits, and the groin. Though there is no cure for hidradenitis suppurativa, early treatment options such as antibiotics, nonsteroidal inflammatory drugs, and immunosuppressant drugs can be helpful in preventing further development of lesions and managing the symptoms. Usually, hidradenitis suppurativa begins during puberty and worsens over time, and occasionally the condition occurs alongside other diseases like Crohn's disease and Graves' disease. Hey, at least it plays well with others.

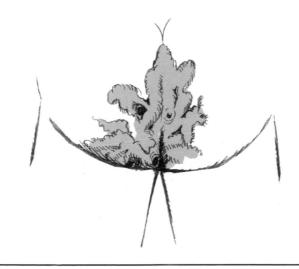

Hidradenitis suppurativa

... have a rash with a red-brown center

You might have a fungal infection related to ringworm called tinea cruris, otherwise known as jock itch. Jock itch is itchy, painful, has blisters or scales at the edges, and usually occurs in the buttocks, the groin, the inner thighs, and in skin folds. While anyone can get jock itch, it is often found in male athletes (hence the name). The fungus responsible for jock itch thrives in steamy and wet environments (such as locker rooms and public showers) and grows best in sweaty workout clothing, damp towels, and wet floors. Jock itch can occur simultaneously with athlete's foot because they are both the result of the same fungus. Just think of jock itch as nature's not-so-subtle hint to wear pants in the gym locker room. That's something we can all be grateful for.

... are red or have pus draining from an abscess

You may have pilonidal disease. This condition, which is more commonly found in men and occurs from puberty to the age of forty, is a skin infection just above the crease between your buttocks. Those affected with pilonidal disease have one or many cysts that usually become inflamed and infected. These cysts usually have a hair sticking out of them and may appear as a small dimple. It is believed that this condition can happen as a result of a hair follicle becoming irritated or a loose hair becoming trapped in the crease of your buttocks, and it's also possible that these cysts were present at birth. If you are not showing any symptoms, there is no need to treat the condition. If, however, the cysts become infected, they may need to be drained, removed, and you may need to take antibiotics. Following treatment, there is a chance that the cysts will return. Essentially, pilonidal disease is your body's way of telling you to say no to crack.

... are bleeding

You may have Crohn's disease (where you have ulcers and swelling of the digestive system), hemorrhoids (swollen veins), an anal fissure (a tear in the lining of the anus), colon polyps (growths in the colon), ulcerative colitis (inflammation and ulcers in the lining of the colon), campylobacter (a type of bacterial food poisoning), or proctitis (an inflammation in the lining of the rectum and anus). Colon polyps are generally harmless and noncancerous; however, these growths can sometimes turn into colon cancer. The most common types of inflammatory bowel disease (or IBD) are Crohn's disease and ulcerative colitis. While ulcerative colitis involves inflammation of the colon and rectum, Crohn's disease can be seen anywhere in the digestive tract, including the mouth and anus. If you have proctitis, this is most likely due to a sexually transmitted disease such as herpes, syphilis, chlamydia, anal warts, or gonorrhea. Blood from your buttocks may be frightening, but so is not knowing what's causing it . . . So get yourself to a doctor, drop trou, and shed some light into the mystery of your black hole.

If you have worms in your stool . . .

You may have some type of parasites inside of you that are most likely either pinworms or ascaris worms, both of which are found more often in children than adults. Pinworms, which are the most common intestinal worm in the United States, can measure up to half an inch. Pinworms live in the digestive system and will actually crawl out of your anus at night while you sleep and lay eggs around the skin folds of the anus. At most, pinworms will cause itching around the anus and restlessness at night. Ascaris worms are much worse. These parasitic roundworms live in the digestive tract as well as the lungs and other organs and cause cramping, diarrhea, vomiting, and, in severe cases, can actually block the intestines. Of course, maybe you have worms because you've been drinking a little too much tequila . . .

. . . have a rash

This can be the result of contact dermatitis, a yeast infection, or even (though rarely) the result of the herpes simplex virus or HIV. Rashes of the buttocks are more common in women than they are in men, and most likely your rash is a result of one of the first two options. A rash from contact dermatitis usually occurs due to the allergens in your underwear, and, generally, these types of rashes form on the buttocks if you sit for too long and sweat (which helps the bacteria grow). If a rash on your buttocks is the result of a yeast infection (which is known as diaper rash when found on babies), this means that the infection began at your genitals and spread to your buttocks. The anus is actually a perfect breeding ground for yeast, which just goes to show you: Some things can never be unread.

Rashes of the buttocks are more common in women . . .

. . . appear dimply, bumpy, or like cottage cheese

You may have the dreaded cellulite, which is caused as a result of the unevenness of the fatty tissue that is beneath your skin and is found more often in women than men. In fact, eight out of ten women have some degree of cellulite on their body. Women are more prone to having cellulite because fat is distributed differently in women (in the hips, thighs, and buttocks). Cellulite is also a result of aging due to the fact that your skin begins to lose some elasticity and is more present when there is weight gain (though lean women can also have it). There are other factors that can lead to cellulite, including genetics, stress, living an inactive lifestyle, and use of hormonal contraceptives. Cellulite is not a serious condition; however, if your boyfriend or husband should ever point yours out, he could end up having one.

... have red breaks in the skin that are oozing

You may have intertrigo, an inflammatory rash that occurs in the skin folds (such as the buttocks, the groin, the armpits, and under the breasts). Intertrigo is caused by bacteria, yeast, fungus, and moisture and is more common in climates that are warm and moist. Keeping the affected area dry, while not the easiest thing to do, will help dramatically, and this can be done with the aid of absorbent fabrics, cottons, or powders. Intertrigo is most commonly found in people who are obese or people who wear medical devices (such as braces, splints, or artificial limbs)—as if they didn't have enough to worry about.

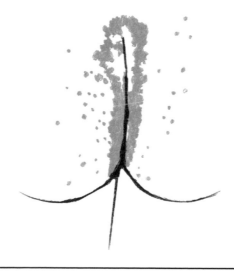

Intertrigo

... have swelling around the anus

You may have hemorrhoids, an inflammation of the veins found in your anus and rectum. Hemorrhoids are commonly caused by straining during a bowel movement and can even be caused by pregnancy (which places more pressure on the veins of your anus and rectum). When hemorrhoids are inside of the rectum, they are known as internal hemorrhoids, and when they are found under the skin and around the anus, they are known as external hemorrhoids. Other symptoms of hemorrhoids include irritation and itching of the anus, a painful or sensitive lump near the anus, leakage of feces, and bleeding while having a bowel movement (though this is not painful). If straining causes an internal hemorrhoid to be pushed through the anal opening, this is known as a prolapsed hemorrhoid. By the age of fifty, around half of the adult population experiences some sort of discomfort or bleeding as a result of hemorrhoids. The other half are stocking up on suppositories in preparation for the big day.

... have a red mass sticking out

You may have a rectal prolapse. This occurs when the rectum stretches out and actually protrudes from the anus. Rectal prolapses are more commonly found in women than they are in men, and they usually occur in children that are six years old or younger and in the elderly. As you get older, the ligaments that hold the rectum in the pelvis stretch, and the muscle of the anal sphincter weakens. A rectal prolapse can develop as a result of a longtime tendency to strain when having a bowel movement, childbirth (from all that pushing during labor and delivery), or a spinal cord disease. Other causes of a rectal prolapse include constipation, cystic fibrosis, a whipworm infection, pinworms, or an injury to the pelvis or anus. People may find your rectal prolapse to be extremely unpleasant to look at, but you'll be a hit among the baboon population.

The rectum stretches out and actually protrudes from the anus.

Sitting all day can be more than just a pain in the ass . . .

It turns out that sitting in a cubicle all day is not only hurting your mental health, it's hurting your physical health. And it doesn't stop there. When you partake in an activity that involves sitting, you are actually shortening your life, and this is something that you cannot make up by exercising. A recent study examined the relationship between mortality and time sitting and found that people between the ages of 50 to 74 who spent their leisure time sitting had a higher mortality rate than those who were more active during their leisure time, and that the rate of death was higher for women than men. Women who reportedly sat for more than six hours a day were 37 percent more likely to die during the 14 year study than women who sat for less than three hours a day, and men who sat for more than six hours a day were 18 percent more likely to die than men who sat for less than three hours a day. So do yourself a favor and get off your ass.

. . . are bruised

You may have injured your tailbone, otherwise known as the coccyx, which is made up of three to five segments of bone that are held together by ligaments and joints. Symptoms of an injured tailbone include a bruise, pain (which is worse when sitting for long periods of time or when pressure is applied to the tailbone), tenderness, and experiencing straining and painful bowel movements. Women are more likely to injure their coccyx due to the fact that the female pelvis is more exposed and broader; if a woman has injured her coccyx, she may also experience pain while having sex. The most common way to injure your tailbone is by a trauma of some sort; however, it can also occur as a result of childbirth and repetitive activities such as bicycling or rowing. So, sitting all day can lead to an injured tailbone, but so can exercising . . . damned if you do, damned if you don't.

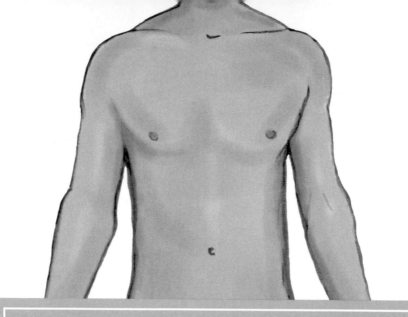

Part 3

The Legs and Feet

Legs • Feet • Toes

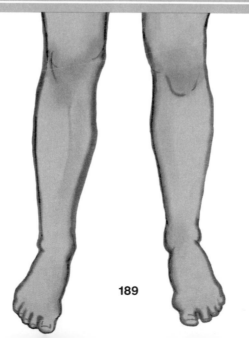

CHAPTER 20

Legs

The bad news: your legs are splotchy, swollen, bumpy, lumpy, and oozing. The good news: you'll have plenty of legroom wherever you go now that everyone is absolutely disgusted by the sight of you. Between your thighs, calves, and knees, the list of possibilities when it comes to illnesses, injuries, and deformities is as long as the legs of a runway model (though, clearly less attractive and sexy). So read up on your symptoms and get a leg up on your condition.

IF YOUR THIGH(S) . . .

. . . are swollen

You may have a thigh contusion. This is an injury commonly found in athletes where the muscle crushes against the bone as the result of an impact. The most common type of thigh contusion is at the front of the leg with the quadriceps. A contusion is also commonly referred to as a "charley horse." However, a severe calf spasm called a charley horse can occur in the middle of the night when you stretch your legs in bed; this can be cured with magnesium. A first-degree thigh contusion features little pain, little swelling, and a mild tenderness of the muscle. A second-degree thigh contusion has a moderate amount

A severe calf spasm [is] called a charley horse . . .

of swelling and pain, and it can be difficult to flex the knee. A third-degree thigh contusion features severe tenderness and pain, and it becomes nearly impossible to flex the knee without having extreme pain. To heal a first-degree thigh contusion, all you need is a little time, an Ace bandage, and ice. For second- and third-degree contusions, you will need crutches. If you are an athlete and you are afraid of getting a thigh contusion, the most successful method of prevention involves running away from physical contact as fast as you possibly can (screaming and arm flailing, while not necessary, certainly does help).

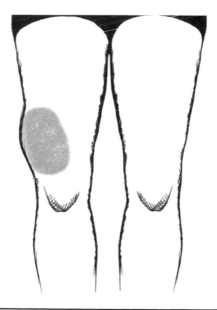

Thigh contusion

. . . has a bruise that moves to the knee and foot

You may have pulled your hamstring, a group of muscles that go from the back of your thigh (starting at the pelvis) all the way to the back of your shinbone below your knee. A pulled, or strained, hamstring is when you have a tear in the hamstring muscle fibers. The degree of your injury can vary, but a severe tear of the hamstring can result in the muscle rupturing, and once you've reached this point, surgery is needed. Symptoms of a pulled hamstring include bruising caused by the small tears in the muscle that bleed, swelling, difficulty flexing the knee, and experiencing muscle spasms. It is important to note that similar symptoms can occur if you have a hamstring contusion. So the next time you're at a party, instead of the played-out "pull my finger" gag, try the new "pull my hamstring!" You'll have everyone's attention as you clutch your leg, fall to the floor, and weep like a small child.

. . . has a lump

This may be the result of an injury or an infection, and, rarely, it is a malignant or benign tumor. Lumps in the thigh can be caused by a bone infection known as osteomyelitis, cellulitis, bone fractures, contusions, strains, or sprains, or they can be a lipoma, a fibroma (a tumor that is benign and made of connective or fibrous tissue), an abscess, a boil, or a hematoma (where blood collects in the tissue). If you have a lump in your thigh and experience a loss of sensation in your leg, coldness in your feet, a weak or absent pulse, paralysis of your leg, or hemorrhaging, you should seek medical attention immediately. In people with long-term osteomyelitis, amputation can be necessary to treat the condition. When in doubt, get your lump checked out!

IF YOUR CALVES . . .

. . . have twisted, bulging, purple, or blue veins

You may have varicose veins. Though these are usually just a cosmetic problem, varicose veins can also cause pain and discomfort, and they can even lead to more serious issues or be a sign of circulatory problems. The veins in your legs and feet are most commonly affected due to the increased amount of pressure standing and walking creates. Common causes of varicose veins include pregnancy, obesity, and simply getting older. As you age, your veins lose their elasticity and begin to stretch, and the valves in your veins weaken, leading to a backward flow of blood (when it should be flowing toward the heart). This causes your veins to pool with blood and enlarge. Varicose veins can sometimes lead to blood clots and ulcers—and they just look fantastic with a skirt or a pair of shorts.

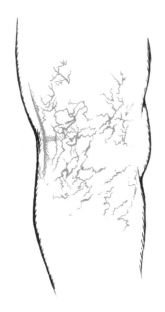

Varicose veins

... are swollen, discolored, and rough in one area

You may be experiencing an inflammatory condition known as stasis dermatitis (where blood pools in the veins of the leg), and you could be developing a stasis ulcer. The pooling of blood causes fluids from the veins to leak into the skin tissue, and this buildup of fluid starts to break down the skin and turn into an ulcer. The skin of the leg surrounding the ulcer may be swollen or discolored, and there may be hard lumps underneath. Stasis dermatitis occurs in women more frequently than men, and it rarely occurs in those under the age of forty. You have a greater chance of developing a stasis ulcer if you are overweight, have varicose veins, have injured your leg in a way that might affect the flow of blood to the veins, and if you have experienced blood clots in your legs previously. As a good rule of thumb, the only time you should want the words "blood" and "pool" in the same sentence is when you're swimming in a pool of Bloody Marys. The hair of the dog might sting a bit, but it's a lot less painful than the open wound in your leg.

You may be experiencing ... stasis dermatitis ...

... are swollen and bruised

You may have a calf strain, an injury commonly found in those who play sports. There are three grades of a calf strain. A grade 1 calf strain consists of mild pain or discomfort, very little to no impact on your mobility, and an aching that occurs two to five days after the injury. A grade 2 calf strain is defined by swelling or bruising, experiencing moderate pain or discomfort while walking, limited ability to do things like running or jumping, and an aching and tightness in the calf for a week or longer. A grade 3 calf strain features significant bruising and swelling, muscle spasms, and severe pain that can make walking impossible. Calf strains usually occur in men between the ages of thirty and fifty. But really, who still plays sports at fifty years old? Who do you think you are? Brett Favre?

. . . have red splotches or patches

This could be the result of a number of things, including poison ivy, poison oak, cholinergic urticaria (hives caused by an increase in body temperature), exercise urticaria (hives brought on by exercise, also known as itchy leg syndrome), heat rash (also known as prickly heat), or a leg heat rash known as golfer's vasculitis. Golfer's vasculitis is not known to many doctors, but people who golf or walk in marathons are very familiar with the rash. It usually starts above the sock line and is seen on the calves. The rash is not itchy and is believed to be caused by prolonged exposure to heat (such as walking in a marathon or playing eighteen holes of golf), which irritates the blood vessels. The main difference between golfer's vasculitis and regular heat rash is that heat rash is itchy and triggered by sweat glands that are blocked. So if you have golfer's vasculitis, you might want to stay off the green for a little bit or suck it up and rent the golf cart; you may look lazy, but at least your rash—and maybe your golf game—will be subpar . . .

. . . have red, tender bumps

You may have an inflammatory condition known as erythema nodosum. The red bumps associated with erythema nodosum are actually a sign that the fatty layer of the skin, the adipose tissue, is inflamed, and these bumps are usually found on the shins. A single bump may last one to two weeks, but new ones can appear for up to six weeks. While erythema nodosum can be an isolated occurrence, it can also be associated with certain disorders and conditions such as sarcoidosis, Behcet's disease, strep throat, pregnancy, inflammatory bowel disease, infectious mononucleosis, and cat scratch disease, and it can even be the result of certain medications like birth control pills. If you have erythema nodosum, you should seek medical attention; while the bumps can be treated easily enough, it's the underlying cause of why you have the condition that you should know more about. Erythema nodosum is more than just a symptom—it's a clue. And your body is the crime scene. Wait, maybe that's not the best analogy . . .

Get muscle cramps often? Try a little lemon in your water . . .

Muscle cramps usually occur in the calves and feet and cause intense pain. Muscle cramps are the result of overuse, strain, injury, sweating out minerals, or remaining in the same position for an extended period of time. While everyone knows that stretching can help prevent muscle cramps, ayurvedic medicine also suggests other techniques including drinking lemon water that has a pinch of salt in it if you have cramps while working out, eating a banana or potato (cooked or baked) or drinking orange juice before you go to sleep, wearing socks that are loose-fitting and warm when sleeping, and creating a ritual an hour before you go to sleep that includes a massage and an Epsom salt (magnesium sulphate) bath, perhaps with candles, music, and dim lighting. You know, having a muscle cramp doesn't sound all that bad, come to think of it . . .

IF YOUR KNEES . . .

. . . are small, deformed, or absent

You have a rare genetic disorder known as nail-patella syndrome. There are many possible symptoms of nail-patella syndrome, including a small, deformed, dislocated, or absent kneecap; discolored, absent, ridged, pitted, split, or underdeveloped nails (fingernails and toenails can be affected, though fingernails are more common, especially the thumb, and instead of a crescent-shaped base of the nail, people with nail-patella syndrome have a triangular shape); and hornlike growths from the pelvis, known as iliac horns. The elbows of a person suffering from nail-patella syndrome may be angled outward or feature webbing, and they may not be able to extend their arms out completely or turn their palms upward while their elbows remain straight. Sufferers are also at greater risk of developing kidney disease and suffering from glaucoma at an early age. Nail-patella syndrome is kind of like being a real-life member of X-Men. Only instead of cool superpowers that can help save the world, you . . . don't get to have kneecaps . . .

. . . have a painful swollen bump

You may have Osgood-Schlatter disease. This disease causes a lump (known as an anterior tibial tubercle) to grow underneath the knee on the upper part of your shinbone. Most often, children who play sports are affected with Osgood-Schlatter disease, and the condition usually goes away when the child is no longer growing. It is believed that the disease occurs from the repeated stress caused by playing sports (such as running, jumping, and quick changes in direction) in kids whose shinbone growth plate is still developing. In Osgood-Schlatter disease, the tendon connecting the shinbone to the knee actually pulls away, and the body may attempt to close this gap by growing a new bone, creating the swollen bump. Sure, your knees may look like the Rockies, but at least you'll have those third-grade soccer trophies that you'll cherish forever . . .

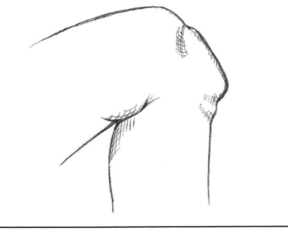

Osgood-Schlatter disease

. . . have a swelling in the back

You may have a Baker's cyst, a buildup of synovial fluid that lubricates the joint of the knee. Baker's cysts form in the back of the knee and can be painless or painful, and can create discomfort and stiffness. If a Baker's cyst ruptures, it may cause bruising and swelling on the calf and the back of the knee. These cysts are usually the result of knee arthritis, rheumatoid arthritis, and a tearing in the meniscal cartilage, which can happen in teens as well as older adults. Usually treatment is not needed, and symptoms will come and go; however, it is important to note that a blood clot can have very similar symptoms, and that needs immediate medical attention. So really, when in doubt, assume the worst.

. . . are popping or clicking

You may have a meniscus tear, otherwise known as a torn cartilage. You have two menisci—made from tough cartilage—in your knee that conform to the bone and are responsible for distributing the weight of your body evenly on the kneecap. The medial meniscus is found inside the knee, and the lateral meniscus is found outside the knee. Due to either degenerative processes or a trauma, you can tear this cartilage. Symptoms of a meniscus tear include pain, swelling of the knee, a clicking or popping sound, tenderness if the meniscus is pressed on, and a limit of motion in the knee joint. Meniscus tears commonly occur with injuries of the medial collateral ligament (MCL) and the anterior cruciate ligament (ACL). When these three problems occur together, this is referred to as the "unhappy triad," which seems like a bit of an understatement. But maybe the "Why-in-God's-name-did-this-have-to-happen-to-me-the-pain-is-unbearable threesome" was too wordy.

. . . are swollen

You may have excess fluid in or around the joint of the knee, which is known as water on the knee. This can occur from a trauma to the knee, or it can be due to an underlying illness or condition. A doctor must take a sample of the fluid to determine the underlying cause of the swelling. Should the fluid have crystals in it, this could be a sign of pseudogout or gout. If bacteria is found in the fluid, this can be a sign of an infection. If blood is found in the fluid, this is a sign of a traumatic injury. Other symptoms of water on the knee include a stiffness of the knee and pain that can be so strong that the knee cannot bear any weight. Certain conditions that can create water on the knee include bursitis, osteoarthritis, rheumatoid arthritis, and tumors. But, honestly, it's not that bad. It's kind of cool to be thought of as the human camel.

are wide apart when you stand with your feet together . . .

This is most likely the result of knee arthritis or the cartilage of the knee joint being worn away. When infants are bowlegged, this is due to diseases such as rickets (which is a weakening and softening of the bones from a deficiency in vitamin D, phosphate, or calcium and magnesium) and Blount's disease (a growth disorder that causes the shinbone to turn inward). Bowlegs are actually normal for children under eighteen months old, and a child is officially considered bowlegged if the condition remains past the age of three. Other causes of bowlegs include bone dysplasias, fluoride or lead poisoning, and fractures that do not heal correctly. If you are experiencing the condition now, it is probably due to arthritis, unless you're a real-life Benjamin Button. But don't get your hopes up; you're probably just old.

IF YOUR ANKLE(S) . . .

. . . have a hard, red cord

You may be suffering from thrombophlebitis, where a blood clot leads to swelling of a vein or veins. This usually occurs in the leg, though it can also appear in the arms and neck. If the swollen vein is closer to the surface of the skin, you may actually see a hard, red cord, and this is a type of thrombophlebitis known as superficial thrombophlebitis. You may develop superficial thrombophlebitis if you have injured your vein or have recently used an intravenous catheter. While another type of thrombophlebitis, known as deep vein thrombosis (spoiler alert: it's the next entry), often shows no symptoms, symptoms of superficial thrombophlebitis are sudden and the inflammation is very visible because there is no muscle for the superficial veins to squeeze. It is for this reason that embolisms rarely occur as a result of superficial thrombophlebitis, or maybe it's just because embolisms aren't shallow enough to hang around with the thrombophlebitis crowd.

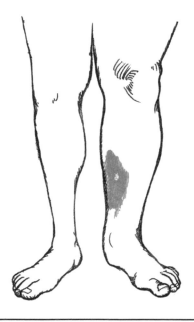

Deep vein thrombosis

... are swollen and pale, red, or blue

You may have a condition known as deep vein thrombosis, another type of thrombophlebitis, where blood clots form in the deep veins found in your body; these veins are usually found in the legs. The condition usually occurs after sitting still for an extended period of time (like a plane flight), and it should not be taken lightly. If a blood clot were to break loose, it could travel through the bloodstream and enter your lungs, leading to a pulmonary embolism. In half of the cases of deep vein thrombosis, no immediate symptoms were present. Some symptoms of a pulmonary embolism include having a rapid pulse, sweating, a sudden shortness of breath, coughing up blood, a chest pain that gets worse when you cough or breathe in deeply, and being nervous or anxious. Then again, that last symptom may be more like a standard of living . . .

. . . is swollen or bruised

You may have sprained it. A sprained ankle happens when the ligaments that are responsible for holding your ankles together either stretch or tear; rolling, turning, or twisting your ankle in the wrong way can cause this sprain and you may experience a limited range of motion with the affected ankle. If you hear or feel a popping as the injury occurs, you may have ruptured or torn the ligament, creating a severe sprain or possibly even a fracture. If your sprain is severe, you may need to use crutches to walk (because putting weight on the affected ankle will be far too painful) or you may possibly need surgery. So the next time you do the twist, make sure you do it right, or you'll be twisting and shouting.

. . . are swollen and your feet are tingling

You may have amyloidosis, a disease where amyloid proteins build up in the organs of your body. Amyloid proteins are abnormal proteins produced by cells in the bone marrow. Amyloidosis can affect different organs and most commonly affects the heart, liver, kidneys, nervous system, spleen, and the gastrointestinal tract. Symptoms of the disease depend greatly on which organ in your body is affected; however, some include swollen ankles, tingling in the hands and feet, an enlarged tongue, feeling weak, purple-colored patches around

Amyloid proteins build up in the organs of your body.

the eyes, weight loss, thickening of the skin or easy bruising, shortness of breath, and an irregular heart beat. There are three major types of amyloidosis: primary (the most common form), secondary (which occurs with inflammatory or infectious diseases), and hereditary (which is inherited). On a positive note, you finally have something to blame your cankles on.

. . . are turned outward

You may have flat feet, which means that the arch on the inside of your foot is flat instead of raised, and that when you stand, your entire foot touches the floor. Having flat feet is usually painless; however, sometimes people with flat feet experience pain in their arches or heels while walking, a swelling in their ankle, and difficulty standing on their tiptoes. Flat feet can also lead to sprained ankles, heel spurs, lower back pain, or hip pain. It can also contribute to arthritis and can cause the feet to turn outward at the ankle. Oftentimes, flat feet are hereditary; however, this condition can also be developed by walking in high heels for extended periods of time, wearing shoes that do not have the proper support, aging, and placing heavy strain on your feet. Note: Having flat feet does not necessarily make you a bad dancer, but any excuse you need is just fine.

. . . are swollen and have yellow, clear, or pink liquid coming out of your pores

This is a sign of extreme edema, a swelling that is the result of excess fluid trapped in the tissues of your leg. Edema can be a premenstrual symptom, and it can be caused by pregnancy, certain medications, too much salt in your diet, and a sedentary lifestyle since movement propels lymphatic tissue. Edema should be taken seriously because it can also be a sign of an underlying illness such as kidney disease, heart disease, and cirrhosis of the liver. Other symptoms include a burning and itchiness of the swollen area, and if you were to press down and create a dimple in your ankle, your skin would retain the impression. Edema is kind of like Memory Foam . . . only grosser.

Clearly, you're just missing gokulakanta and cow urine in your diet

Are your legs swollen from edema? Do you wish more than anything that you could fix the problem? Do you find yourself asking "What should I do with all of this cow urine?" Well, question no more, my friend, because you are in for a treat. Ayurvedic medicine offers several remedies for your fluid retention problem, and the solution can be found by using various herbs including belleric myrobalan, kantakari (which also acts as a diuretic), black nightshade, and the ash of gokulakanta. Taking the ash of gokulakanta is much more effective if you pair it with cow's urine. Which makes sense if you think about it. I mean look at all of the classic pairings: white wine and fish, red wine and pasta, beer and nuts, and gokulakanta and cow urine. Nope. Nothing strange about that . . .

. . . has a swelling that gets progressively worse throughout the day from activity

You may have Achilles tendinitis (or swelling of the Achilles tendon). The Achilles tendon is actually the largest tendon found in the body, and it connects the heel bone to the calf muscles. There are two types of Achilles tendinitis: insertional Achilles tendinitis and noninsertional Achilles tendinitis. In insertional Achilles tendinitis, the lower part of the heel is affected, and often bone spurs will occur as a result. In noninsertional Achilles tendinitis, the middle part of the tendon is affected; this type of Achilles tendinitis is degenerative and affects younger and active people more often. Other symptoms of Achilles tendinitis include a thickening of the tendon, stiffness and pain in the morning, severe pain twenty-four hours after exercising, and pain in the back of the heel that gets worse as you become more active. Looks like computer geeks, gamers, stoners, and couch potatoes get out of this one scot-free.

Do your ankles get swollen when you fly?
While this is usually not a very serious condition and can happen to anybody, it can lead to very serious complications. Your ankles become swollen due to an accumulation of fluid from not moving your legs for an extended period of time. This can lead to the development of a blood clot, and if this lodges in a vein and breaks, you can suffer from an embolism, which can ultimately lead to death or damage to the vital organs. People who are obese or overweight are more likely to have swollen ankles while flying and are more likely to develop blood clots. To prevent ankle swelling, try wearing support stockings, or flex and stretch your ankles, calves, and feet periodically. So the next time you're on a long flight, take a walk around the plane between the in-flight movies.

CHAPTER 21

Feet

Do you take stinky feet to a whole new level? When you hear the word "corn," does your mind automatically hoof it down to your toes? Understanding the underlying cause of your foot problems is not only incredibly important, but it will also help get you off on the right foot in terms of treatment. Most importantly, be sure to learn the cause of your symptoms sooner rather than later. That way, you don't end up six feet under . . .

IF YOUR FEET . . .

. . . are cracking and peeling

You may have athlete's foot, a fungal infection caused by dermatophytes and closely related to ringworm and jock itch. Other symptoms of athlete's foot include itching blisters; a burning, itching, and stinging sensation between the toes and on the soles of your feet; extremely dry skin at the bottom and sides of your feet; and thick, discolored, and crumbly toenails that move away from the nail bed. Men, those who wear tight shoes or damp socks, and those who walk barefoot in public spaces (such as locker rooms, swimming pools, showers, etc.) are at the greatest risk of getting athlete's foot. Unfortunately, you don't even have to be an athlete to take this trophy home.

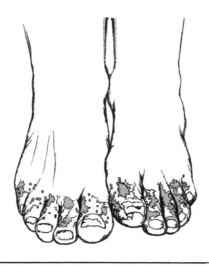

Athlete's foot

. . . have blotchy and cold skin

Take those damp socks off and let your feet dry off for a little while, because you may have trench foot. Trench foot, also known as immersion foot, was common among soldiers fighting in the cold, wet trenches during World War I, and it occurs when a person's foot stays wet for an extended period of time. Symptoms of trench foot include an itching or tingling sensation, pain, swelling, numbness, blotchy and cold skin, leg cramps, and a slow or even stopped pulse in the affected foot. Necrosis can set in as tissue dies, and fungal infection adds to the mess. Blisters may also form, which can cause tissue and skin to die and fall off, and if left untreated, the entire foot can be affected leading to gangrene. If the foot is warmed, it will typically feel painful and dry. To prevent trench foot, keep your feet dry—and don't assassinate any archdukes; you won't regret it!

. . . have pitted, white patches of skin

You probably have a bacterial infection known as pitted keratolysis. The condition is caused by several different species of bacteria that thrive in moist environments, and it commonly affects those who have very sweaty feet. While pitted keratolysis can be itchy, the most noticeable symptoms are the white patches of pitted skin that appear on pressure-bearing sites like the heel or balls of the feet and a very strong odor that is actually the result of sulfur compounds that the bacteria produce. Pitted keratolysis can also show up on the palms of the hands. The infection can be treated with antibiotic creams or medications; however, there is a chance that it will recur if you do not keep your feet dry. In addition to any medication, you should wear socks that absorb sweat, put antiperspirant on your feet twice a day, wash your feet with antiseptic cleanser or soap twice a day, and always carry smelling salts—so that you can wake anyone who passes out from the odor.

. . . have hard, thick sections of skin

You may have corns or calluses, which develop in areas where pressure is applied when the skin attempts to protect itself from this pressure and friction. Corns are much smaller than calluses. In corns, there is a hard center, and the surrounding skin is inflamed. Corns can cause pain and will usually develop on parts of the feet where not too much weight is placed on them. Calluses, on the other hand, do not hurt, vary in shape and size (but are usually larger than corns), and develop on the soles. Common causes of corns and calluses include wearing shoes or sandals without socks (which creates friction), wearing socks that do not fit, and wearing shoes that are too loose, too tight, or have high heels. How can you get rid of your corns? You guessed it: start husking!

Get rid of your corn with a little garlic . . .

Do you love to cook? Are you sick of your nasty-looking corns or calluses? Are you into trying alternative medicine? Well, here's some ayurvedic instruction for you:

- **Step 1:** Roast a clove of garlic (in a type of butter known as ghee or just dry) until it is golden brown.
- **Step 2:** While the clove of garlic is still warm, apply it to your corn or callus and cover it up with a Band-Aid. You should use a clove of garlic for every corn. Leave these on for a day.
- **Step 3:** Repeat. Do this every day until the corn or callus falls off.
- **Step 4:** Massage your feet with a rejuvenation massage oil to make sure your skin is soft and to prevent corns or calluses from growing back.
- **Step 5:** Apologize to everyone you know for having to put up with your stench.

. . . are turned downward and inward

You (but more likely your child) may have clubfoot. Foot deformities caused by clubfoot are usually present at birth, and it can range from mild to severe and affect one or both feet. The condition is known as clubfoot because the angle of the foot in relation to the ankle resembles that of the head of a golf club.

In some cases, a foot can be turned so much so that it appears upside down. Clubfoot also leads to underdeveloped calf muscles, the affected foot may be shorter than the nonaffected foot, and it can hinder your child's development when it comes time to learn how to walk. Despite its unsightly appearance, clubfoot does not cause any pain or discomfort. Studies have shown that there is a link between smoking during pregnancy and clubfoot, but if you're smoking while pregnant, you need a club to the head in some way or another.

. . . have small lesions on the sole

You may have what are known as plantar warts. Plantar warts are noncancerous growths of the skin and are actually caused by the human papillomavirus (HPV). The virus enters the body through small breaks or cuts in the feet, and the warts usually develop on the balls or heels of the feet, where a greater amount of pressure is applied. Other symptoms of plantar warts include black pinpoints (known as wart seeds), a callus over a spot where a wart grows inward, and experiencing pain while standing or walking. While there are hundreds of different types of HPV, only a few can cause plantar warts. Plantar warts will usually go away on their own, but it can take up to several years, and they can be very stubborn to treatment. HPV and stubborn to treatment? Plantar warts sure sound like a lot of the young celebrities running around Hollywood these days.

Plantar warts are noncancerous growths of the skin . . .

. . . lose their muscle

You may suffer from Charcot-Marie-Tooth disease, which is actually a group of disorders that affect the peripheral nerves.

Charcot-Marie-Tooth disease is inherited, and it creates muscle weakness and a decrease in the bulk of the arm and leg muscles. The condition usually starts in the feet and legs, and high arches and hammertoes are common symptoms. While the symptoms range in severity, they will often get worse over time and move past the legs and feet, affecting the hands and arms. Other symptoms of Charcot-Marie-Tooth disease include weak ankles, feet, and legs; loss of muscle in the legs as well as the feet; difficulty moving your feet or walking; experiencing less sensation or numbness in your legs and feet; and frequently falling down or tripping. Symptoms usually occur during adolescence or early adulthood, but signs of the condition can also start showing up later on in life. Finally, a disease clumsy people can grasp onto (and hold on tight).

... drag as you walk

You may have foot drop, which is a term used to describe when a person struggles to lift the front of his or her foot due to it being weak or paralyzed. Foot drop is not a disease but rather an indication of an underlying anatomical, neurological, or muscular problem. Foot drop is commonly caused by a compression of the peroneal nerve (which is responsible for controlling the muscles that lift the foot) at the knee or lower spine. Compression of this nerve can occur from crossing your legs, wearing a cast, and kneeling for a prolonged amount of time. Foot drop can also be the result of long-time nerve damage caused by diabetes, or it can be the result of muscular dystrophy, Charcot-Marie-Tooth disease (discussed in the previous entry), polio, multiple sclerosis, amyotrophic lateral sclerosis (ALS), stroke, or wearing extremely heavy boots.

CHAPTER 22

Toes

Are you tired of constantly having to be on your toes? Are you sick of making sure your pedicure matches the blue, black, purple, red, or brown coloring that's starting to appear down there? Does your hammertoe look like it belongs inside of a toolbox instead of a sneaker? If this sounds like you, it's time to put the *fun* back in *fungus* and start figuring out exactly what's wrong! So stop tiptoeing around the subject and start reading! It might just save your life—or, at the very least, bring your flip-flops out of retirement.

IF YOUR TOE(S) . . .

. . . have a red, calloused, bony bump

You might have a bunion, a bump that forms at the base of your big toe's joint, forcing your big toe to push against the other toes. As time goes on, the bunion becomes bigger, crowding the rest of the toes even further and leading to pain. While there are many causes of bunions, the most common cause is from wearing shoes that are too tight (such as high-heel shoes that are narrow-toed); this happens because the pressure from standing is not evenly distributed among the joints and tendons, and the big toe joint becomes unstable, molding a part of it into a knob that sticks out. While a bunion affects your big toe, you can actually have small bunions on the joints of your little toes, and these are known as bunionettes. Chances are that given the shoes and the dance numbers, the Rockettes have a few "Bunionettes" on stage with them.

... looks clawlike or hammerlike

You may have hammertoe or mallet toe (yes, very inventive names here). Hammertoe is when your toe is bent at the middle joint, curling the toe, and a mallet toe is when your toe curls due to a bend at the upper joint. Shoes with high heels or shoes that are too tight in the toe area commonly cause the unnatural bend of your toe by forcing the toe against the shoe. For extreme cases of hammertoe and mallet toe, surgery may be needed to correct the condition. Hammertoe and mallet toe can be painful, and moving the toe can be difficult. This condition can be frustrating to live with—especially if your friends call you insensitive nicknames like M. C. Hammertoe or Gene Mallet.

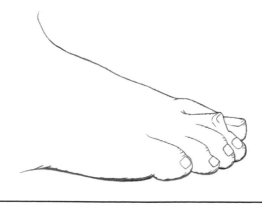

Hammertoe

...is oozing

You may have an ingrown toenail. While any nail on your toes can become an ingrown nail, the nail of the big toe is usually the most common. The early stages of an ingrown toenail include pain, swelling, and redness. During the next phase, skin and tissue will form around the nail, which may lead the toe to ooze a yellow-colored discharge. It is important to know that this is not necessarily an infection but rather the body's response to the skin being irritated by the nail. Should the toe become infected, the swelling will worsen, the toe may ooze a white or yellow drainage, and there is the possibility that you may develop a fever. If not treated, an ingrown toenail can even lead to an abscess. Wearing tight shoes, not cutting your toenails properly, having injured your toe, a fungal infection of the nail, and even a family history of ingrown toenails put you at a greater risk of having ingrown toenails. On the bright side, if you ever walk barefoot along the beach, you'll always be able to find your way back to your towel by following the trail of ooze . . .

> An ingrown toenail can even lead to an abscess.

...has a swelling at the base or ball of the big toe

This might be a sign of a condition known as turf toe, which is a sprain of the ligaments that surround the joint of the big toe. Turf toe is most often found in athletes—especially football players—and dancers. It commonly happens to those who play or perform on artificial surfaces such as turf, where players' cleats stick to the ground more than they would on grass. For example, if a player runs very quickly and then stops abruptly, the shoe stops moving because of the turf, but the toe hits the inside of the shoe, causing the sprain. The injury is usually very sudden, and there is sometimes a popping sensation. Turf toe can really be a problem for football players who celebrate after getting a touchdown. So that's why they put that excessive celebration penalty in place . . .

. . . are blue or black

You may have blue toe syndrome (well that seems simple enough). Blue toe syndrome is also known as trash foot (this just gets better and better) and is the result of a lack of blood flow to the toes. Blue toe syndrome most commonly occurs when—during an angiography or foot, cardiac, or vascular surgery—a piece of arterial plaque breaks off in the arterial system of the stomach and groin, travels to the foot via the arteries, and becomes lodged, eventually turning into an embolism. Due to the lack of oxygen, the tissue that is in front of this blockage becomes a color that ranges from blue to black. In the worst cases of blue toe syndrome, gangrene can occur, which leads to amputation of the affected toes. Other causes of blue toe syndrome include scleroderma, diabetes, Raynaud's phenomenon, and drawing a sad face on each of your toes.

. . . overlap or underlap

You may have deformities of the foot that might require surgery. Underlapping toes curl under the other toes, and this usually occurs with the fourth and fifth toes. Though why this occurs remains unknown, it is believed that these toes underlap due to an imbalance in muscle strength of the small muscles inside the foot. When toes overlap, one toe lies on top of another toe, and it is usually the fifth toe that is affected. It is believed that overlapping toes may be a result of the position of the fetus in the womb, and there is also a hereditary component involved. In both cases, surgery can sometimes correct the condition by releasing the soft tissues and tendon of the joint. In more severe cases, a pin (which can stay in for up to three weeks) can be inserted to straighten the toe. It is also entirely possible that your toes just want to snuggle with each other, in which case breaking them apart will make you a cold, heartless bastard (but a cold, heartless bastard with normal-looking toes).

... are black, purple, brown, or red and have a foul smell

You may have gangrene, the death of body tissue as a result of a bacterial infection or a lack of blood flow. Most often, the toes, fingers, and limbs are affected by gangrene, though it also occurs in the internal organs, muscles, and even the genitals. There are many different types of gangrene, and the color of your wound depends on which type you have. Dry gangrene, which features shriveled, dry skin, develops slowly and turns your skin black, brown, or a purplish blue. Wet gangrene, which can be fatal, is a bacterial infection that features blistering, swelling, and a wet appearance. Another fatal type of gangrene, gas gangrene, features gray or purplish red, bubbly skin, that when pressed upon may make a crackling sound due to a release of gas. The most important thing to take away from this discussion is that, as you head out to the hospital, make sure your wardrobe doesn't clash with the color of your wound, or you'll get picked up by an ambulance—and the fashion police.

... have crumbly nails

You may have onychomycosis, or to put it simply, nail fungus. An infection caused by fungus in the nail can take on many different appearances due to what type of fungus you have, though general symptoms of nail fungus include toenails that are thickened, crumbly, ragged, brittle, distorted, dark in color, or without shine. Onycholysis is when an infected nail actually separates from the nail bed, and there may be a foul odor and pain. The fungi most commonly found in nails are dermatophytes; however, mold and yeast can also create fungal infections of the nail. Nail fungus can sometimes be hard to treat, and infections can recur. To prevent this condition, always keep your toenails clean, dry, and trimmed; wear socks that keep your feet dry (such as synthetic socks over cotton or wool); wash your hands after you have touched a nail that has fungus (because it can spread); wear shoes in public places like showers, pools, and locker rooms; and under no circumstances should you ever play footsie.

. . . have a pink, scaly patch in between the skin folds

You may have a bacterial infection known as erythrasma, which features a scaly or wrinkled, pink or red rash that has clearly defined edges. This skin condition is most commonly found between the third and fourth toes but also can be seen in other areas where there are skin folds, such as the armpits, under the breasts, and on the groin (it is rarely seen on the buttocks). Erythrasma is sometimes mistaken for jock itch due to the color and location of the infection. As time progresses, however, one can tell the difference between erythrasma and jock itch because the rash caused by erythrasma can become brown in color, while the rash caused by jock itch or other fungal infections is typically always pink in color. To treat erythrasma, you can take antibiotics or use an antibacterial soap. People who are elderly, overweight, diabetic, or reside in warm and moist climates are at a greater risk of getting the infection. Seems like erythrasma is the nonjock's jock itch.

Is your second toe longer than your big toe?

If so, then you have a Morton's toe, which is seen in about 10 to 20 percent of the population. While a Morton's toe is not a sign of any condition or illness, it can cause pain. Because the second toe is longer, this is the toe that is going to take the impact and pressure from each step you take. This can lead to the formation of a callus and black toenail (when a blister forms underneath the toenail bed, turning it black). Having a Morton's toe can also cause you to walk with overpronation, where your foot turns more inward after it lands from each step. Morton's toe is sometimes called Greek toe because it is seen in many of the ancient Greek statues, as well as the Statue of Liberty, which was modeled after the style of the ancient Greeks. If you have a Morton's toe, find the right shoes, make sure you always lace them properly so your feet don't move around, buy orthotics if you need to, or just make like the ancient Greeks and suck it up.

Abdominal swelling, 153–54
Achilles tendinitis, 204–05
Acid reflux, 27
Acne keloidalis nuchae, 16–17
Acoustic neuroma, 41
Acromegaly, 124–25
Acupuncture, 115
Age spots, 99
Alien hand syndrome, 127
Allergic reactions, 141
Allergic rhinitis, 49
Alopecia areata, 9–10, 32
Amyloidosis, 202–03
Anaphylaxis, 141
Angioedema, 21
Angular cheilitis, 52–53
Ankles, 200–205
Ankylosing spondylitis, 101–02
Anxiety, 17
Areolas, 145
Arms, 105–20
Arthritis, 116, 126, 130, 131, 177, 200
Ascaris worms, 183
Athlete's foot, 206–07
Atopic eczema, 15
Ayurvedic medicine, 18, 26, 37, 47, 60, 119, 137, 144, 176, 196, 204, 209

Back, 96–104
Bacterial vaginosis, 172
Bad breath, 57–58
Baker's cyst, 198
Balanitis, 165–66
Balanoposthitis, 165–66
Baldness, 10
Barrel chest, 140
Bartholin cysts, 176–77
Basal cell carcinoma, 16
Beau's lines, 134
Bedbugs, 75–76
Bedsores, 96–97
Bell's palsy, 26–27
Belly button, 156
Biceps, 105–06
Birthmarks, 72–74
Black dermographism, 88
Blaschko's lines, 102

Bleeding, 50, 85, 136–37, 173–74, 182–83
Blepharitis, 32, 33
Blepharospasm, 30–31
Blinking, 30–33
Blisters, 15, 41–42, 51–52, 63, 78, 86–87, 97, 126–27, 133
Bloating, 154
Blocked tear ducts, 35
Blue toe syndrome, 215
Boutonniere deformity, 130–31
Bowlegs, 200
Bradykinesia, 108
Breast cancer, 144, 149
Breast implants, 145–46
Breasts, 143–51
Broken arm, 111
Broken heart syndrome, 142
Bubonic plague, 67
Budd-Chiari syndrome, 155
Buerger's disease, 132
Buffalo hump, 91–92
Bulimia, 10
Bullous pemphigoid, 86–87
Bunions, 212–13
Bursitis, 94–95
Buttocks, 180–88

Café au lait spots, 72
Calf strain, 194–95
Calluses, 208–09
Calves, 193–96
Cancer
  breast, 144, 149
  cervical, 173, 174
  endometrial, 174
  kidney, 99
  nasal cavity, 48–49
  oral, 55–56
  prostate, 163
  skin, 16, 23, 70–71
  testicular, 166–67
  thyroid, 64–65
  vulvar, 175
Candida, 53–54
Canker sores, 53
Carpal bossing, 118
Celiac disease, 158
Cellulite, 184

Cerumen impaction, 40–41
Cervical cancer, 173, 174
Cervicitis, 174
Chagas disease, 34
Charcot-Marie-Tooth disease, 210–11
Charley horse, 190–91
Cherry hemangioma, 88
Chest, 138–42
Chilblains, 133–34
Chlamydia, 164, 170
Chondritis, 43
Chronic obstructive pulmonary disease (COPD), 140
Churg-Strauss syndrome, 112
Cicatrical alopecia, 9–10
Clubfoot, 209–10
Coccyx, 187–88
Cold sores, 51–52
Colon polyps, 182–83
Conjunctivitis, 35–36
Constipation, 152–53
Contact dermatitis, 184
Corns, 208–09
Crabs, 167–68
Cranial nerve palsy, 31–32
Crohn's disease, 157, 182, 183
Cushing's syndrome, 91–92
Cutaneous horns, 82
Cyanosis, 124

Dandruff, 13–14
Deep vein thrombosis, 200–202
De Quervain's tendonitis, 117
Dermatomyositis, 79
Deviated septum, 45–46
Diabetes, 58, 115
Dislocated shoulder, 93
Distal biceps tendon rupture, 105–06
Doshas, 47
Dry skin, 19–20
Dupuytren's syndrome, 122
Dyshidroticsis eczema, 126–27

Ears
  hearing loss, 41
  infections, 38–39, 41–43
  redness, 39
  ringing, 40–41
Eating disorders, 10
Eczema, 15, 88, 107, 126–27
Edema, 20, 203–04
Ehlers-Danlos syndrome, 84
Elbows, 112–15
Embolism, 205
Endometrial atrophy, 174
Endometrial cancer, 174
Endometrial hyperplasia, 173–74
Erectile dysfunction, 169
Erections, 168–69
Erythema nodosum, 195–96
Erythrasma, 217
Eyebrows, 32
Eyelashes, 32
Eyelids, 32–33
Eyes, 28–36

Face, 19–27
Feet, 206–11
Female genitals, 162–63, 170–77
Fever, 67–68
Fibrocystic breast condition, 143–44
Finger clubbing, 134–35
Fingernails, 134–37
Fingers, 129–37
Fish scale disease, 113
Flat feet, 203
Foot drop, 211
Fractures, 111
Frostbite, 135
Frozen shoulder, 95
Fusarium, 30

Ganglion, 123–24
Gangrene, 216
Gastroenteritis, 155–56
Genitals
  female, 162–63, 170–77
  male, 164–70
Genital warts, 170–71
Gingivitis, 56

Gluten, 158
Goiter, 65–66
Gokulakanta, 204
Golfer's vasculitis, 195
Gonorrhea, 164–65, 170
Gout, 126
Granuloma annulare, 115
Grave's disease, 66
Grover's disease, 84–85
Gynecomastia, 149–50

Haemolacria, 29
Hair
  chemically treated, 12
  discolored or depigmented, 12
  dry and brittle, 10
  falling out, 8–10
  premature gray, 11–12
  thicker, 10–11
  unusual growth of, 11
Hammertoe, 213
Hamstring pulls, 192
Hands, 121–28
  blue, 124
  deformed, 122
  enlarged, 124–25
  involuntary movement, 127
  lumps, 123–24
  swollen, 121–22
Hashimoto's disease, 66
Hay fever, 49
Head size, 23
Hearing loss, 41
Hemorrhoids, 185–86
Hepatic vein obstruction, 155
Hepatitis, 83, 120
Hernias, 160–61
Herpes, 26–27, 51–52, 133, 175, 184
Herpetic whitlow, 133
Higradenitis suppurativa, 180–81
Hip dysplasia, 177–78
Hips, 177–79
Hirsutism, 11
Hives, 21, 141
Human papillomavirus (HPV), 170–71, 173, 210

Hunchback, 100–101
Hyphema, 28–29
Hypoparathyroidism, 10
Hypothyroidism, 10, 20

Ichthyosis vulgaris, 113
Impetigo, 78
Inflammatory bowel disease, 183
Ingrown toenail, 214
Intertrigo, 185
Intussusception, 152–53
Iron deficiency, 12
Itching, 14, 17, 32, 63, 78–79, 80, 85, 86, 126, 183

Jaundice, 82
Jaw spasms, 58–59
Jock itch, 181–82, 217
Jogger's nipple, 151

Karsch-Neugebauer syndrome, 132
Keloids, 17
Keratoacanthoma, 22–23
Kerions, 18
Kidney cancer, 99
Kidney imbalance, 11–12
Klippel-Trenaunay-Weber syndrome, 75
Knees, 197–200
Koro syndrome, 166
Kyphosis, 100–101

Lateral epicondylitis, 113–114
Legs, 190–205
Leukoplakia, 54–55
Lice, 167–68
Lichen nitidus, 141
Lichen planus, 120
Lichen sclerosus, 172–73
Lipomas, 91
Lordosis, 98
Lumps, 32–33, 55–56, 64–65, 91, 99, 109, 118, 123, 143–44, 149, 160–61, 165, 176–77, 192
Lupus, 25
Lyme disease, 97–98
Lymphatic filariasis, 108–09

Lymphedema, 106–07
Lymph nodes, 62–63, 67, 106–07, 169–70
Lymphogranuloma venereum (LGV), 169–70

Madarosis, 32
Madelung's deformity, 115–116
Malassezia furfur, 14
Male genitals, 164–70
Malnutrition, 157
Mammary duct ectasia, 146–47
Marfan syndrome, 129–30
Mastitis, 148–49
Mastoiditis, 42
Melanoma, 16, 70–71
Melasma, 24–25
Meningitis, 67–68
Meniscus tear, 199
Moersch-Woltman Condition, 100
Moles, 70–74
Mongolian blue spots, 73–74
Morgellons disease, 86
Morton's toe, 218
Mouth
    bad breath, 57–58
    blisters or lesions, 51–52
    clicking, 55
    cracks, 52–53
    gums, 56–57
    infections, 53–54
    tongue color, 60–61
    ulcers or sores, 53, 55–56
Muir-Torre syndrome, 22
Multiple sclerosis, 24
Muscle cramps, 196
Muscle twitching, 109–10
Myasthenia gravis, 31, 36
Mydriasis, 31

Nail fungus, 216–17
Nail-patella syndrome, 197
Nasal cavity cancer, 48–49
Nasal polyps, 44–45
Neck
    lumps, 64–65

rash, 63
stiffness, 67–68
swollen, 62–63, 65–67
twisted, 64
Neurodermatitis, 88
Neurofibromatosis, 41, 72
Nipple discharge, 146–48
Nipples, 151
Norovirus, 156
Nose
    broken, 46
    congestion, 44–46, 48–49
    discharge, 47–48
    runny, 49
Nosebleeds, 50
Nummular dermatitis, 107

Onychomycosis, 216–17
Oral cancer, 55–56
Osgood-Schlatter disease, 197–98
Osteoarthritis, 116
Osteomyelitis, 192
Otitis externa, 39–40
Otitis media, 38–39
Overlapping toes, 215–16

Paget's disease, 147
Palm lines, 128
Paralysis, facial, 26–27
Parasites, 34, 75, 78–79, 86, 108–09, 155, 159, 172, 183
Parkinson's disease, 32, 108
Patterson-Stevenson syndrome, 132
Pectus carinatum, 139–40
Pectus excavatum, 138–39
Pelvic congestion syndrome, 162
Pelvic inflammatory disease (PID), 162–63
Pelvis, 160–79
Pemphigus, 52
Penis, 165–66, 168–69
Perichondritis, 42–43
Perifolliculitis capitis abscedens et suffodiens (PCAS), 15–16
Periodontitis, 56–57

Petechiae, 85
Peyronie's disease, 165
Phosphorus, 10
Photophobia, 29–30
Pilar cysts, 16
Pilondial disease, 182
Pinworms, 183
Pitted keratolysis, 208
Pityriasis capitis, 13–14
Plantar warts, 210
Poland syndrome, 150–51
Port-wine stains, 74
Posture, 104
Pregnancy, 10–11, 24, 80, 145, 162, 186
Priapism, 168
Prolactinoma, 147–48
Prostate cancer, 163
Protein deficiency, 12
Proteus syndrome, 125
Pruritic urticarial papules and plaque of pregnancy (PUPPP), 80
Pseudomonas folliculitis, 163–64
Psoriasis, 14–15, 17, 88
Pubic lice, 167–68
Pulse, 119
Pupils, dilated, 31
Pyoderma gangrenosum, 87

Ramsay Hunt syndrome, 41–42
Rashes, 25, 41–42, 63, 75–81, 163–64, 181–82, 184, 185, 195
Raynaud's phenomenon, 27
Rectal prolapse, 186
Rectocele, 171
Renal cancer, 99
Rheumatoid arthritis, 130, 131, 177
Ringworm, 18, 76, 181–82
Rocky Mountain spotted fever, 80
Rosacea, 22

Scabies, 75
Scalp, 13–18
Scalp folliculitis, 15–16
Scarlet fever, 59

Scars, 16–17
Scleroderma, 27
Scoliosis, 103
Seborrheic dermatitis,
    14–15
Seborrheic keratosis, 16, 17
Separated shoulder, 94
Sexually transmitted dis-
    eases (STDs), 164–65,
    167, 169–71
Shingles, 41, 76–78
Shoulders, 90–95
Sinus infection, 47–48
Sister Mary Joseph nodule,
    156
Sitting, 187
Skin
    blisters, 86, 126–27
    blue, 124
    bumps on, 86, 89, 115,
        120, 141, 163–64
    itchy, 88
    moles, 70–75
    patches, 81–82, 172–73,
        217
    rashes, 25, 41–42, 63,
        75–80, 163–64, 181–
        82, 184, 185, 195
    scaly, 113
    spots, 85
    stretchy, 84
    ulcers, 87
    yellow, 82, 155
Skin cancer, 16, 23, 70–71
Slipped epiphysis, 179
Snapping hip syndrome,
    178–79
Spasms, 118
Splinter hemorrhage,
    136–37
Split-hand deformity,
    132–33
Sporotrichosis, 109
Sprained ankle, 202
Squamous cell carcinoma,
    16, 23
Stasis dermatitis, 194
Stenosing tenosynovitis,
    136
Stiff person syndrome, 100
Stomach, 152–59

Stomach flu, 155–56
Stress, 8–9, 17
Sturge-Weber syndrome, 74
Stye, 32–33
Swan neck deformity, 131
Swayback, 98
Swelling, 121–22, 133–34,
    141, 153–55, 169–70, 177,
    190–91, 198, 199, 203–05
Swimmer's ear, 39–40
Swimmer's itch, 78
Symmastia, 145–46
Synesthesia, 43
Syphilis, 167

Tailbone, 187–88
Tapeworm, 159
Telogen effluvium, 8–9
Temporomandibular joint
    disorder (TMJ), 55
Tendonitis, 117
Tennis elbow, 113–114
Testicular cancer, 166–67
Testosterone, 11
Tetanus, 58–59
Thigh contusion, 190–91
Thighs, 190–92
Thinness, 156–58
Thrombophlebitis, 200–201
Thrush, 53–54
Thumb tendonitis, 110, 117
Thyroid cancer, 64–65
Thyroid disease, 10, 20,
    65–66, 116
Tibial aplasia, 132
Tinea cruris, 181–82
Tinea versicolor, 81
Toes, 212–18
Tongue, 60–61
Torn cartilage, 199
Torticollis, 64
Transcutaneous electrical
    nerve stimulation (TENS),
    95
Tremors, 110–11
Trench foot, 207–08
Trichomoniasis, 172
Trichotillomania, 32
Trigeminal neuralgia, 23–24
Trigger finger, 136
Tumors, 41, 123, 124, 156

Turf toe, 214–15
Twitching, 109–10

Ulcerative colitis, 12
Ulcers, 87, 96–97, 194
Underlapping toes, 215–16
Urine testing, 176

Vagina, 171, 175, 176–77
Vaginal discharge, 162–63,
    170, 172
Vaginitis, 172
Varicose veins, 162, 193
Virilization, 11
Vitiligo, 82
Von Willebrand disease
    (vWD), 50
Vulvar cancer, 175

Warts, 170–71, 210
Water on the knee, 199
Weight loss, 156–59
Winged scapula, 92–93
Worms, 108, 159, 183
Wrist, 115–20

Xanthelasma palpebrarum,
    33

Yeast infections, 53–54,
    172, 184
Yips, 118–19

Dear reader,

Thank you for putting on your rubber gloves and venturing outside to purchase this book. It's in a safer place now.

About the Author

As a self-described neurotic and self-diagnosing hypochondriac, it didn't take long for **Paul Kleinman** to realize his true calling in life—helping complete strangers experience as much panic and paranoia as he does. In fact, during the writing process, Paul was able to self-diagnose at least seven skin conditions and nine illnesses (all of which turned out to be nothing). Paul's work has been featured on McSweeney's and he is the author of *The Bullsh*t Artist* and *A Ton of Crap.* Paul currently lives in New York, NY, in an apartment he is almost positive has black mold.

About the Technical Reviewer

Carolyn Dean, MD, ND has been in the forefront of the natural medicine revolution since 1979. She is the author/coauthor of twenty-three health books including *The Magnesium Miracle, The Yeast Connection and Women's Health, Death by Modern Medicine, The Everything® Alzheimer's Book,* and *Hormone Balance.* Dr. Dean has a free newsletter, a valuable online wellness program called Completement *Now!,* and a busy telephone consulting practice. She is also the medical director of the Nutritional Magnesium Association, and lives in Kihei, HI. Learn more at *www .drcarolyndean.com.*

IN CASE OF EMERGENCY

Name: _____ Date of Birth: _____

Hospital Preference: _____ Insurance Company: _____

Primary Care Physician: _____

Allergies: _____

Emergency Contacts

Name: _____ Relationship: _____

Home Address: _____

Telephone: _____ Cell: _____

	Name	**Number**
Pathologist:		
Oncologist:		
Neurologist:		
Anesthesiologist:		
Ophthalmologist:		
Otolaryngologist:		
Rhinologist:		
Allergist:		
Dietitian:		
Stomatologist:		
Dentist:		
Orthodontist:		
Periodontist:		
Dermatologist:		
Plastic Surgeon:		
Cardiologist:		
Pulmonologist:		
Endocrinologist:		
Orthopedic Surgeon:		
Gastroenterologist:		
Nephrologist:		
Obstetrician/Gynecologist:		
Proctologist:		
Urologist:		
Podiatrist: